Music Library Association
Basic Manual Series

Jean Morrow, Series Editor

1. *Music Classification Systems,* by Mark McKnight, edited by Linda
Barnhart, 2002.

Music Classification Systems

Mark McKnight

Music Library Association
Basic Manual Series, No. 1

The Scarecrow Press, Inc.
Lanham, Maryland, and London
and
The Music Library Association
2002

SCARECROW PRESS, INC.

Published in the United States of America
by Scarecrow Press, Inc.
A Member of the Rowman & Littlefield Publishing Group
4720 Boston Way, Lanham, Maryland 20706
www.scarecrowpress.com

4 Pleydell Gardens, Folkestone
Kent CT20 2DN, England

British Library Cataloguing in Publication Information Available

Library of Congress Cataloging-in-Publication Data

McKnight, Mark Curtis, 1951–
    Music classification systems / Mark McKnight.
        p. cm.—(Music Library Association basic manual series ; no. 1)
    Includes bibliographical references (p.) and index
    ISBN 0-8108-4262-9 (alk. paper)—ISBN 0-8108-4263-7 (pbk. : alk. paper)
        1. Classification—Music. 2. Cataloging of music. 3. Classification—Sound
recordings. 4. Cataloging of sound recordings. I. Title. II. Series.

ML111 .M45 2002
025.4'678—dc21   2001057702

⊗™ The paper used in this publication meets the minimum requirements
of American National Standard for Information Sciences—Permanence of
Paper for Printed Library Materials, ANSI/NISO Z39.48-1992.
Manufactured in the United States of America.

For my father, and in memory of my mother.

Contents

Foreword

With the publication of *Music Classification Systems*, the Music Library Association launches a comprehensive series of manuals intended to address various aspects of dealing with the organization, administration, and use of a music library. This series will form the core of any music librarian's working library, providing assistance both to the novice as well as the experienced librarian, and benefiting both public librarians and academic librarians in the humanities who have music in their collections.

The authors for this series represent senior members of the music library profession who bring a wealth of knowledge and practical experience to their manuals. Forthcoming titles will include *The Binding and Care of Music, Library Instruction, Music Reference, The Acquisition of Music Materials*, and *Media Equipment*.

Editorial Board:
Linda Barnhart
Deborah Campana
David Hunter
Peter Munstedt
Jean Morrow, Series Editor

Acknowledgments

I thank the Music Library Library Association and its Publications Committee, and specifically Linda Barnhart and Jean Morrow, for inviting me to write this manual. These two individuals have been wonderfully supportive and have provided much practical and editorial advice throughout the project. A number of other colleagues also need to be recognized for their assistance: Brad Young, Jean Harden, Catherine Sassen, and Ralph Hartsock offered suggestions and answered a number of questions I had on technical matters related to music classification. Dean Jensen and Peter Brown provided expert guidance on DDC and ANSCR classification details, and Eddie Tealer gave me invaluable assistance with creating the flowcharts.

Figures

CHAPTER 1

An Introduction to Music Classification

The organization and arrangement of music materials in libraries has long presented special challenges for librarians and others entrusted with the custody and care of those materials. Such challenges have centered on a variety of factors, chief among them, the distinctive nature of music as a separate "language" that nonmusicians might not be able to read or understand. Sometimes librarians with relatively little expertise in music find themselves having to deal with it—whether in circulating music materials, cataloging and providing access to those materials, or assisting users who need information about music. As a result, music often gets shoved aside into the cataloger's "problem" pile, or those complicated music reference questions receive less-than-satisfactory answers. The purpose of this manual is to relieve the "stress" level for general catalogers with no special background or knowledge of music by providing some practical guidelines in the classification of music materials and to clarify and explain the most commonly used classification systems in the United States, the Dewey Decimal Classification (DDC), the Library of Congress Classification (LCC), and The Alpha-Numeric System for Classification of Recordings (ANSCR).

One of the differences between music and other library materials is the wide variety of physical formats in which it is found. Handel's *Messiah*, for example, could appear as a full score (either with Handel's original Baroque instrumentation or with a more "modern" orchestration), as a vocal score with piano or organ accompaniment, as a score of only the chorus parts or solos, or as a score of excerpts or selections. It could be published in the original English language, or in any number of different translations. And there is also the issue of recordings, which include anything from reel-to-reel tape recordings of local productions to vintage 78-rpm commercial releases, to cassettes, LPs, or compact discs. Librarians need some expertise in or special knowledge of all these differences in order to provide adequate access to music.

Such distinctions go to the heart of defining what music itself *is:* is it the notes on the printed page, the sonic recreation of those notes, or something else altogether? Although our aim here is not to pose some philosophical debate, nevertheless, the differences in various manifestations of music do have some bearing on the practical need to arrange it in a meaningful way that fulfills the fundamental function of a library's particular organization and purpose.

Materials in most libraries are organized according to schemes that place like topics or subjects in the same physical location (the browsing or collocating function in bibliographic control theory)—users want to see all the books a library has on French Impressionist painting, stockcar racing, or dinosaurs, all together on the shelf. The key difference music has from most other types of library materials is this "aboutness"; although much music might have some kind of topical facet or characteristic (a tone poem by Richard Strauss or the latest rap song), libraries have traditionally treated music more abstractly, choosing to focus on the form or genre of a musical work or the instrumentation of that work, rather than on any extramusical meaning it might convey. People who use libraries usually expect to find all of the piano music, opera scores, or popular song folios in the same location, rather than all of the music inspired by the ocean, or all of the works relating to Christmas, regardless of their instrumentation. In fact, even if they want specific items, most users more often than not ask instead for directions to a general location ("Where is your trumpet music?"—if they want the Hummel trumpet concerto, or "Where are your hymnals?"—if they are really only looking for "How Great Thou Art"). Perhaps this is related to the way modern Americans shop in retail stores—most people like to browse and see what else might be available, even if they have a specific item in mind to purchase.

Another problem music presents is its complexity. Organizing all of the piano music or hymnals together on the shelf is fairly simple and straightforward, but what about music written for more than one instrument, or music materials that contain a number of different kinds of works (e.g., an anthology of music by various composers or a sound recording that contains many different pieces)? Such complexities require not only knowledge of music, but also a fundamental understanding of the principles of library classification. In his book *Organising Music in Libraries*, Brian Redfern discusses these dilemmas and observes that "Whatever knowledge is brought to the problem of organising music in a library, there must be a solution which will provide an order on the shelves making sense to the users of the library and arranging material in a helpful and systematic way."[1] For those nonmusical librarians who continue to be daunted or overwhelmed by the perplexing nature of music, Redfern notes that, regarding the classification or arrangement of music, "there is some evidence to suggest that, certainly as far as devising a scheme for arrangement is concerned, a good grounding in classification principles may be of more value."[2] Music librarians and others in the profession might want to debate Redfern's assertion, arguing that it is much easier to teach a musician cataloging than to train a cataloger to be a musician (even the rudiments of music are probably too complicated or time-consuming to include in a cataloger's curriculum). Be that as it may, it is, as Redfern notes, important for librarians to be informed about general principles of classification, especially as they relate to music.

What is equally important, and sometimes overlooked, is the "differentness" of music libraries and collections, one from another. Libraries grow organically and develop according to the particular needs of their constituencies as well as the individual imaginations of those who arrange them. This is especially true in older libraries that have been in existence for years before the advent of online bibliographic utilities, which have imposed so much greater uniformity among libraries in general. In academic institutions, especially those with small music departments, music collections might be minimal (a few hundred scores and sound recordings) and be run under the aegis of the music department, separate and apart from the main library, and headed by someone with no formal library training. Many of these organizations have operated adequately by storing printed music and recordings in files or bins arranged alphabetically by composer and medium. Often, in time, these collections get transferred to the institution's library, which might have no one with the requisite musical training or background to handle them.

Many institutions have developed in-house marking systems or have adapted existing schemes in general use for their own circumstances. This is particularly true for collections of sound recordings. Writing in 1963, Gordon Stevenson noted that of 392 libraries responding to a survey, only 37 replied that their systems were known to be based on those of other libraries.[3] The 392 libraries in the survey reported a broad array of ways of organizing and classifying their recordings, all of which are viable and acceptable, as long as they meet the needs of the library and its users. Libraries organize their recordings in some of these ways:

- Accession number
- Manufacturer's number
- Adaptation of Dewey D.C.
- Adaptation of L.C.
- Arrangement by broad subject area
- Color code used as location symbols
- Schedules with a letter notation
- Arrangement in alphabetical order, by composer, author, or title
- Other systems[4]

A number of factors determine how items are arranged on the shelf, but perhaps the chief one for music, and especially sound recordings, is where the items are shelved, either in open or closed stacks. In general, public libraries tend to have open stacks with more liberal lending policies, and academic institutions more usually keep recordings in closed stacks and restrict borrowing of these items, although this practice seems to be changing among many institutions. Libraries that house recordings in open stacks are generally more likely to have some sort of arrangement that permits meaningful browsing (a classification scheme), whereas libraries with closed stacks can get by with shelving by accession or manufacturer's number (the amount of available storage space is also a factor here). Stevenson reported that of the 302 libraries in his survey that had either open or partially open stacks, 200 (66 percent) utilized some sort of classification system, although these systems represented great variety in their structure and organization.[5]

The advent of compact discs has forced many libraries to limit public access to recordings because CDs are smaller and easier to steal than LPs. Libraries have gotten around the theft problem in creative ways, by placing empty CD containers in public browsing areas while keeping the actual discs in a secure location, or by providing browsing of CD inserts or accompanying booklets, again keeping the discs stored behind the desk. This practice allows the library to maintain its classification system and still permits browsing of the library's holdings while holding shrinkage to a minimum.

Although libraries have devised many clever and creative ways of organizing music materials, it should be noted that none of these systems is completely perfect or without drawbacks. The particular system a library adopts should be carefully thought out with the specific needs of its users in mind, and not just for the convenience of the staff or person in charge of the collection. Arrangement by accession number is, of course, the easiest from a number of perspectives (simpler to catalog and shelve), but it is perhaps not the best way to organize materials in an open-stack environment. Conversely, libraries that have small collections and keep some or all of their materials in closed stacks are probably wasting valuable staff time if they decide to use a classified organization scheme, although one might argue that *virtual* browsing (i.e., in the online catalog) by call number is also a benefit to users, particularly to those who access the library's catalog from a remote location. Again, all of these factors should be considered in deciding what kind of access is to be provided for the library's music materials.

MUSIC CLASSIFICATION—HISTORY AND BACKGROUND

Two developments in the nineteenth century contributed to the rise of music librarianship and the concomitant need to devise schemes for organizing music. One of these developments was the establishment of public libraries in the U.S. and Great Britain as institutions deemed necessary for the social and cultural well-being and benefit of communities; the other was the gradual inclusion of music as an academic discipline in institutions of higher learning in the U.S. and abroad. The latter development coincided with the birth and rise of musicology as a recognized field of scholarly endeavor, first on the European continent and then in Great Britain and the United States.

Of the former, American public libraries gradually began to include music as part of their circulating collections throughout the last quarter of the century. Brooklyn Public Library was the first American library to offer music for circulation to the public. W.A. Bardwell described this collection in an April 1887 issue of *Library Journal*.[6] Bardwell explained that, in 1882, one of the directors of the library supplied funds for the purchase and binding of four hundred volumes "selected from the best writers of music, classical and modern" (including, in addition to such predictable names as Mozart, Beethoven, Schubert, and Mendelssohn, such lesser lights as Raff, Gade, and Pauer). Bardwell deemed the experiment a success, stating that "if an opera is to be produced, or if the Philharmonic Society has on its programme selections from any of the noted composers, there is directly a call for the work thus brought to notice." He observed that, just as library patrons often checked out books to examine for possible addition to their own collections, so too did the circulation of musical scores allow "musical people . . . an opportunity of examining and practising at home and at leisure compositions that require examination, and thus ascertaining whether or not they are desired as purchases."[7] The music collection at Brooklyn was so successful that it had almost doubled by the time Bardwell wrote his article for the *Library Journal*. Bardwell also stated that a bulletin of the whole collection had been printed for users, and he described the classification of the collection, which was divided into two main categories, "*First, Instrumental Music*" and "*Second, Vocal Music.*" Each main category was subdivided, and these subdivisions strongly reflect the role music played in the average middle-class American household—categories under "Instrumental Music" included the following:

1. Piano solo (two hands)
2. Studies and exercises for two hands
3. Overtures for two hands
4. Scores for two hands
5. Piano duets (four hands)
6. Overtures for four hands
7. Scores for four hands
8. Two pianos (eight hands)
9. Harmonium (cabinet organ)
10. Full scores

Under the heading "Vocal Music" are the following categories:

1. Songs
2. Vocal duets
3. Oratorios, cantatas, masses, odes, choruses, anthems, etc.
4. Operas, music and words[8]

Ten years after Bardwell's article appeared, James Duff Brown, Librarian of the Clerkenwell (England) Public Library, published in the British journal *The Library* guidelines for cataloging music. Brown's system is similarly straightforward and, like the Brooklyn Public Library system, reflects very much the musical culture of his day; it also demonstrates clearly the basic principles of organization and access that are still the hallmarks of sound librarianship today: "Under the main subject-heading 'MUSIC,' I recommend an entry of every musical work in the library, arranged according to the scheme set out below. Cross-references can be made from the body of the catalogue to each specific head. It will facilitate finding if arbitrary numbers are applied to the different sections."[9] Brown's classification system is strictly numeric and consists of forty-two categories in a sequence ranging from (1) "*General.*—Criticism, &c." through (2–7) "History" and "Theory" to (8–29) "Practice, Instrumental" (each category devoted to a different instrument), to (30–42) "Practice, Vocal" (each category representing a different type of vocal music from opera to songs, ballads, and "nursery music"). Each of the instrumental categories is subdivided into "(a) Instruction or History" and "(b) Music for" (thereby placing the books about the topic in proximity with the printed music for the instrument). Interesting is the fact that the individual instrumental categories are arranged alphabetically, beginning with "American Organ" and ending with "Violoncello." In addition to the standard instruments one would expect to find in such an arrangement from this time, also included are categories for the banjo and concertina. The different divisions of vocal music, from "Church Services, Masses" through "Songs [etc.]" are also subdivided (a) and (b), but in this instance (a) is "Collections" and (b) is "Individual Composers," reflecting the tendency of many of these types of works to be published in collections and anthologies.[10] Brown stresses the importance of providing adequate information to the user in regard to instrumentation because a "pianoforte score of an opera or overture is a very different thing from a full score, which in its turn is quite another thing from the separate parts for each instrument. The nature of each work should therefore be clearly described."[11]

Music libraries in institutions of higher education in the United States began to develop in the late nineteenth century. It was not until the first half of the twentieth century, however, that academic music libraries began to be more common. Many of these libraries developed their own systems of cataloging and access, in part modeled on the practices and systems of the main libraries of their institutions, and in part on the special profile and function of each individual collection. In a 1902 issue of *Library Journal*, Clarence W. Ayer described the classification system in use in the Harvard College Library, a system he devised, based on the work of another library classification pioneer, Charles Ammi Cutter (1837–1903), whose Expansive Classification was used at the Boston Athenaeum and at Forbes Library in Northampton, Mass. Ayer explained that his system was designed with "gaps after all important groups, which will allow ample provision for growth for at least ten years to come."[12] Ayer's system was numeric and consisted of three main sections: I. Works on Music (Mus. 1–400); II. Collections (Mus. 401–600); and III. Individual Composers (Mus. 601–895).[13]

SYSTEMS OF CLASSIFICATION

In *Introduction to Cataloging and Classification* (7th ed. by Arlene G. Taylor), Bohdan S. Wynar discusses the history of traditional classification schemes. Library classification systems date back to the earliest civilizations. The great Alexandrian library of the third century B.C. is known to have had a catalog devised by the poet Callimachus, organized by subject and subdivided by author. Although the library and its catalog were later destroyed, they served as the model for a number of bibliographies and catalogs in the Byzantine Empire and the Middle East until the Middle Ages.

Libraries of the great medieval European universities arranged their books according to the traditional seven subjects taught, which were organized as the Trivium and the Quadrivium. Books in these libraries had fixed locations on the shelves; classification was arranged through book catalogs that provided access to the shelf location. This fixed-location system was maintained by most European and early American libraries until well into the 1800s.[14]

As Wynar notes, the history of classification in modern libraries "corresponds to the various attempts to adapt and modify existing philosophical systems of knowledge to the arrangement of materials and to users' needs."[15] He cites Thomas Jefferson as one who, early on, adapted portions of Francis Bacon's outline of knowledge to his own library as well as the libraries of the University of Virginia and the College of William and Mary. Bacon's outline was also used as the basis for organizing other libraries during the period, including those at Harvard and the College of South Carolina, as well as the famous French Enlightenment landmark by Denis Diderot and Jean Le Rond d'Alembert, the *Encyclopédie ou Dictionnaire raisonné des sciences, des arts et des métiers* (1751–1765). William Torrey Harris (1835–1909), librarian of the St. Louis Mercantile Library, was a follower of the German philosopher Georg Wilhelm Friedrich Hegel (1770–1831); he inverted Bacon's system of knowledge to create, as Wynar calls it, an "independent American classification."[16] It was this system that served as the basis for Melvil Dewey's classification scheme, which he first devised in 1876.

Although many music libraries have been very creative in devising their own systems of classifying and organizing music, a number of different classification systems have also been written throughout the years by various persons attempting to bring some kind of uniformity and consistency to music collections and to assist librarians in dealing with the difficult problem of making materials easily available to library users. Some of these systems for music classification are part of larger library classification schemes, such as the Library of Congress and the Dewey Decimal systems, the two most frequently used arrangements found in libraries. Other schemes have been designed specifically for music materials. Among these systems is the Dickinson System, devised by librarian and music scholar George Sherman Dickinson for use at the Vassar College Music Library and adopted by a number of libraries in the northeast United States. The Dickinson system is musicologically based, designed for study rather than performance-oriented collections. Another system, used more frequently in Britain than the U.S., is the McColvin Classification, published in 1924 by Lionel McColvin and designed as a revision of the Dewey 780s (the numeric range for music in the DDC). McColvin intended his system as a rectification of what he and many others recognized as a major flaw in the DDC, the lack of distinction between music and literature about music.[17] Many other libraries that use DDC have modified it in various ways to allow for these distinctions.

The introduction of sound recordings to library collections during the middle years of the twentieth century posed a serious dilemma for librarians as they struggled with ways to make these new formats accessible to users. The Alpha-Numeric System for Classification of Recordings (AN-SCR) was developed specifically to answer the problem of inadequate access to recordings under existing classification systems. It is still used in a number of libraries today and has many virtues to recommend it, particularly for circulating collections.

Although a thorough and detailed examination and evaluation of all of the existing classification systems for music would be enlightening, this book focuses on the three systems most commonly used in American libraries today: the Dewey Decimal Classification system (DDC), the Library of Congress Classification System (LCC), and ANSCR.

NOTES

1. Brian Redfern, *Organising Music in Libraries*, vol. *1, Arrangement and Classification*, Rev. ed., (London: Clive Bingley; Hamden, Conn.: Linnet Books, 1978), 10.

2. Ibid., 9–10.

3. Gordon Stevenson, "Classification Chaos," *Library Journal*, October 15, 1963; reprinted in *Reader in Music Librarianship*, ed. Carol June Bradley (Washington, D.C.: Microcard Editions Books, 1973), 274.

4. Ibid., 274–275.

5. Ibid., 275.

6. W.A. Bardwell, "A Library of Music," *Library Journal* 12 (April 1887): 159.

7. Ibid.

8. Ibid.

9. James Duff Brown, "Cataloguing of Music," *The Library* series 1 (1897): 82; reprinted in *Reader in Music Librarianship*, ed. Carol June Bradley (Washington, D.C.: Microcard Editions Books, 1973), 144.

10. Ibid.

11. Ibid., 145.

12. Clarence W. Ayer, "Shelf Classification of Music," *Library Journal* 27 (January 1902): 6.

13. Ibid., 6–7.

14. Bohdan S. Wynar, *Introduction to Cataloging and Classification*, 7th ed. by Arlene G. Taylor (Littleton, Colo.: Libraries Unlimited, 1985), 369.

15. Ibid.

16. Ibid., 370.

17. For a more detailed discussion and comparison of the Dickinson and McColvin systems with DDC and LCC, see Olga Buth, "Scores and Recordings," *Library Trends* 23 (1975): 427–450.

CHAPTER 2

Dewey Decimal Classification (DDC)

HISTORY AND BACKGROUND OF DDC

When Melvil Dewey (1851–1931) first published his *Classification and Subject Index for Cataloguing and Arranging the Books and Pamphlets of a Library* anonymously in 1876, he conceived it to be like earlier systems that were Baconian-based. Dewey attempted to organize all of knowledge; therefore, his scheme reflects a philosophical orientation that differentiates it from the Library of Congress Classification System, which is based on the principle of literary warrant (i.e., it only covers the subjects that a library actually includes in its collection). DDC has been criticized throughout the years for reflecting its author's own biases and beliefs and for lacking objectivity, but despite these criticisms, it has remained remarkably resilient, principally because it is continually revised and updated.

Novel and revolutionary about Dewey's approach were its decimal organization and its relative index, both of which allowed for expansion as new fields of knowledge developed. Although some earlier systems did use decimals, they were used as fixed-location markers or as accession numbers. Dewey's system, on the other hand, permitted libraries to maintain their collections in relative, rather than fixed locations so that like items could remain together on the shelf.

Dewey was a young assistant librarian at Amherst College in 1873 when he began to look for a more efficient method for arranging books in the Amherst library. He visited more than fifty libraries and studied writings on library management (called "library economy" at the time). Dewey later wrote about his findings in a 1920 *Library Journal* article on the origins of DDC (Dewey's concern with economy and efficiency is also reflected in his use of phonetic spellings—including that of his own first name, which he shortened from Melville to Melvil):

> I was astounded to find the lack of efficiency, and waste of time and money in constant recataloging and reclassifying made necessary by the almost univer-

sally used fixt [sic] system where a book was numberd according to the particular room, tier, and shelf where it chanced to stand on that day, insted of by
class, division and section to which it belonged yesterday, today and forever.[1]

Dewey's solution to the problem was certainly clever, and we might
even consider it as divinely inspired—in his preface to the first edition
of DDC (1876), he describes how the idea came to him while attending
church one Sunday:

> After months of study, one Sunday during a long sermon by Pres. Stearns, while
> I lookt stedfastly at him without hearing a word, my mind absorbd in the vital
> problem, the solution flasht over me so that I jumpt in my seat and came very
> near shouting "Eureka"! It was to get absolute simplicity by using the simplest
> known symbols, the arabic numerals as decimals, with the ordinary significance
> of nought [i.e., 0], to number a classification of all human knowledge in print.[2]

Dewey's decimal-based concept has worked surprisingly well during
the 125 years of its existence, considering the tremendous changes
every aspect of civilization has witnessed during this time. The flexibility of the schedule and its ability to be updated periodically have permitted DDC to maintain its position as the leading system of library
classification in the U.S. and many other countries.

The Dewey Decimal Classification is published by Forest Press, now a
subsidiary of OCLC Online Computer Library Center, Inc. In order to
maintain its currency it is constantly being updated—the latest edition of
the system, DDC 21, appeared in 1996. It is now available in both print
and electronic form, including the World Wide Web. Through what are
known as "Phoenix" schedules, the system (or various classes therein)
has occasionally undergone a complete overhaul—this allows the schedule to remain current, though it does at times pose the necessity for reclassification of older materials to maintain unity of collocation and pre-
vent shelf dislocation. One of the latest such revisions occurred when the
editors decided to overhaul the music portion (780–789) of DDC with the
twentieth edition (1989).[3] This decision stemmed from longstanding con-
troversy and unhappiness with Dewey's treatment of music by many librarians whose libraries use DDC for their collections.

From the outset, many people have argued, the schedule for music in
DDC was inadequate (although perhaps a little more specific than the
Brooklyn Public Library plan). Following is the overall schedule for
music in the first edition of DDC:

780   Music.
781   Theory.
782   Dramatic.
783   Church.
784   Vocal.
785   Instrumental.
786   *Piano and Organ.*
787   *Stringed instruments.*
788   *Wind*   "
789   Associations and institutions.[4]

One of the main reasons for librarians' unhappiness with DDC's treatment of music has been that it does not adequately separate music from books about music. Only within each class are scores given a separate sequence. This system clearly is not adequate for most libraries who prefer to keep scores and books in separate sections within their collections.

DDC has also been widely criticized for failing to keep abreast of new developments in music and for not sufficiently covering music of non-Western cultures or Western popular idioms. A look at the schedule for music in DDC 19 demonstrates how little it had changed from the first edition, published more than a hundred years earlier:

780   Music
781   General principles
782   Dramatic music
783   Sacred music
784   Voice & vocal music
785   Instrumental ensembles & their music
786   Keyboard instruments & their music
787   String instruments & their music
788   Wind instruments & their music
789   Percussion, mechanical, electrical[5]

General dissatisfaction with the system caused many librarians in DDC-classed libraries to look for other systems in which to organize their music collections. For example, the University of Illinois at Urbana-Champaign, which has one of the largest Dewey-classed libraries, converted to LCC for its music and sound recording collections a number of years ago. Many British libraries adopted the McColvin adaptation of Dewey, which does separate books and scores. A large number of U.S. libraries have solved the score-vs.-book problem by placing a prefix (usually M) in front of the Dewey class number for scores, so that a volume of piano music falls under M786.2, while books on piano music keep the original numeric designation 786.2. Libraries that classify recordings similarly place an R or some other mnemonic prefix before call numbers for their recordings. These types of call numbers are still found today on items in many libraries that long ago switched from DDC to LCC and did not retrospectively reclassify older materials (a situation that sometimes creates confusion for library users and novice shelving assistants).

Many of the earlier complaints about DDC's treatment of music were rectified with the twentieth edition. One of the main improvements in DDC 20 is that after more than a hundred years and nineteen previous editions, it finally acknowledges and allows for distinctions between music and books about music. Still, it is unlikely that libraries that had elected to adopt other systems will revert to DDC; the revision, however, does represent great improvement for libraries that use DDC for music and should result in an increased level of satisfaction for catalogers as well as users of those libraries.

Another of the traditional criticisms of DDC, that it was biased in favor of Western art music, was also addressed in the Phoenix revision. As the manual states, it was "imperative that the new schedule for music be hospitable to the music of all cultures. Thus it was essential to find a value-free basis for the classification of instruments."[6] In order to accommodate this objective approach and give equal emphasis to instruments of non-Western cultures, the editors applied the principles of organization outlined in the "Systematik der Musikinstrumente; ein Versuch," by Erich M. von Hornbostel and Curt Sachs, which appeared in the *Zeitschrift für Ethnologie* 4–5 (1914).[7] This system arranges musical instruments according to their acoustic properties into four broad classes—aerophones, idiophones, membranophones, and chordophones. The system was altered in DDC 20 by placing keyboard and mechanical instruments into primary classes, and by adding a fifth category for electronic instruments (electrophones).[8]

ARRANGEMENT WITHIN DDC

The DDC is currently published in four volumes. The first volume includes an introduction and the classification tables; volumes 2–3 contain the various schedules; and volume 4 consists of the manual and relative index. At the beginning of volume 2 are listed three summaries outlining the classification schemes in order from general to specific. The first summary lists the ten broad categories or main classes of the overall system, within the ranges 000 to 900. The ten main classes include the following:

000	Generalities
100	Philosophy & psychology
200	Religion
300	Social sciences
400	Language
500	Natural sciences & mathematics
600	Technology (Applied sciences)
700	The arts
800	Literature & rhetoric
900	General geography & history[9]

Each of these ten main classes is further subdivided into ten sections (*divisions*), described in the second summary. Music is found in the main class 700, The arts, the ten divisions of which are:

700	**The Arts**
710	Civic & landscape art
720	Architecture
730	Plastic arts Sculpture
740	Drawing & decorative arts
750	Painting & paintings
760	Graphic arts Printmaking & prints
770	Photography & photographs
780	Music
790	Recreational & performing arts[10]

Each division is then divided into ten parts (*sections*):

780	**Music**
781	General principles & musical forms
782	Vocal music
783	Music for single voices The voice
784	Instruments & instrumental ensembles
785	Ensembles with one instrument per part

786   Keyboard & other instruments
787   Stringed instruments (Chordophones)
788   Wind instruments (Aerophones)
789   [see below][11]

It is rather remarkable that, within the range of only ten whole numbers (780–789), a whole spectrum of library materials relating to music can be classified in some kind of meaningful and logical arrangement—from the works of medieval composer Adam de la Halle to books on zydeco, or from a recording of ABBA's greatest hits to the theoretical treatises of Zarlino. It is the use of decimals and relative numbers, of course, that makes this possible, a plan that permits the system to expand for future developments, and, as we have stated, keeps like items together on the shelf.

DDC's decimal organization also allows it to be both hierarchical and faceted. By *hierarchical*, we mean that the numbers within it proceed from general to specific according to discipline and subject matter. Only in the ten main classes does this hierarchical force not apply. Hierarchies may represent various relationships, such as whole-part, genus-species, or increased specificity. These hierarchical relationships are explained in the following paragraphs (p. 23ff.).

In DDC 20, the class numbers for music, the 780s, are divided into three major parts (780–781, for Generalities; 782–783, for Vocal music; and 784–788 for Instrumental music), plus an optional number for composer and traditions of music (789). Within both vocal music and instrumental music, the progression is from large to small: orchestras and bands comprise 784, chamber music (one person per part) 785, and works for one instrument 786–788. The primary subdivisions for music within DDC 20 are:

780.1–9   Standard Subdivisions
781   General principles and musical forms
781.1   Basic principles
781.2   Elements
781.3–.4   Techniques
781.5–.6   Kinds and Traditions of music
781.7   Sacred music
781.8   Forms
782–783   Vocal music
782.1–.9   Opera and choral

783	Single voices
784–788	Instruments and their music
784	Orchestras and bands
785	Ensembles with only one instrument per part
786–788	Specific instruments and their music
786	Keyboard, mechanical, electrophonic, percussion
787	Stringed
788	Wind
789	[Composers option]
789.2–.9	[Traditions of music option][12]

The last section, 789, which provides an option for placing individual composers and traditions of music, is new with DDC 20, and represents one of the major changes in the revision from DDC 19 and earlier editions, which place percussion music in this section.

NOTES AND INSTRUCTIONS

Trying to read and interpret the DDC can be daunting. Fortunately, the editors have included a manual (vol. 4) as well as notes and instructions within the schedules that provide guidance and, in many instances, explain and clarify the captions in the schedules. These notes are used in a variety of circumstances and comprise several different categories, including notes that describe what is found in a class, notes on what is found in other classes, see-manual notes, and number-building notes.[13]

Definition Notes

A definition note is found below a heading and gives the meaning of the term. Definition notes are used in three different instances: (1) the heading is either narrower or broader than commonly understood; (2) the heading either has more than one meaning or is ambiguous (based on definitions in general unabridged dictionaries); or (3) the term is new to the language.[14]

Ex.:
781.286	Counterpoint
	Two or more independent melodic lines

786.69   Aeolian instruments
              Instruments activated by the blowing of the wind

Scope Notes

Scope notes give the limits under which the heading can be used, either by limiting or broadening it.

Ex.:
782.1   Dramatic vocal forms   Operas
              Regardless of type of voice or vocal group [broadens the scope]

782.323 2   Common (Ordinary) of the mass
              Contains Kyrie, Gloria, Credo, Sanctus, Benedictus, Agnus Dei [narrows the scope]

Variant-Name Notes

Variant-name notes also help define what is included under a heading by giving alternative names (i.e., synonyms) for the heading.

Ex.:
786.55   Reed organs and regals
              Variant names for reed organs: American organs, cabinet organs, harmoniums

Class-Here Notes

The schedules provide class-here notes quite frequently to list or explain major topics to be included in a class, even though the topics listed may be narrower or broader than the heading. Class-here notes are prescriptive, and the topics can be other terms or ways of interpreting the same concept.

Ex.:
781   General principles and musical forms
              Class here music theory

782.25   Sacred songs
          Class here small-scale sacred vocal forms

785   Ensembles with only one instrument per part
          Class here chamber music

Including Notes

In DDC, some topics have what is called "standing room," which means that they are included as part of a class number, even though they can be narrower in scope than the heading represented by that class number. They are placed with, or included with, the class because there are relatively few works written about them, although more literature about them could appear in the future. If that occurs, they will be assigned their own class numbers. Topics represented as standing room cannot have numbers from standard subdivisions, or other number-building techniques, applied to them.

Ex.:
780.262   Manuscripts
          Including autograph scores, sketch books

781.654   Mainstream jazz
          Including swing

784.182 6 Paraphrase forms
          Including musical parody

Class-Elsewhere Notes

As the name implies, these notes may be considered as the opposite of class-here and including notes. Similar to see references, they instruct as to where interrelated topics are located. According to Chan, class-elsewhere notes "are used to show preference order among topics, to lead to broader or narrower topics in the same notational hierarchy to override the first-of-two rule, or to lead to the comprehensive or disciplinary number for the topic."[15] A class-elsewhere note is given in the form of "class . . . in . . . ." In some instances, class-here and class-elsewhere notes can be found together.

Ex.:
780.216   Lists, inventories, catalogs of music
             Class here thematic catalogs
             Class thematic catalogs of individual composers in 780.92

783.1   Single voices in combination
             Class here part songs
             Class music intended equally for choral or part-song per-
             formance in 782.5

Comprehensive-Works Notes

This type of note is related to the class-elsewhere note and applies to topics that can be found within more than one class within a discipline.

Ex.:
780.269   Stories, plots, synopses
             . . . .
             Class comprehensive works in 782.00269

781.286   Counterpoint
             Two or more independent melodic lines [definition note]
             Class comprehensive works on harmony and counterpoint in
             781.25

Comprehensive-works notes are also found for centered-entry topics. Centered-entry topics are indicated by an arrow (>) and represent a broad topic covered by a range of numbers. This kind of note is used for topics that cover all aspects within the center-entry range.

Ex.:
>   781.63–781.69   Other traditions of music
                      . . . .
                      Class comprehensive works in 781.6

>   782.23–782.29   Specific sacred vocal forms
                      Class comprehensive works in 782.22

See References

As with class-elsewhere notes, see references refer from one class number to a subordinate part of the topic that has its own class number. This type of note is printed in italics and is given in the form *"For . . ., see . . . ."*

Ex.:

| 781.237 | Intervals |
| | *For consonance, see 781.238; dissonance, 781.239* |

| 782.2 | Nondramatic vocal forms |
| | *For secular forms, see 782.4* |

See-also References

See-also references are given in the same format as see references. They refer to other topics that may relate in some way to the given heading.

Ex.:

781.62   Folk music

. . . .

See also 780.9 for music of and performed in a specific location

786.59   Electronic organs

. . . .

See also 786.74 for synthesizers

Revision Notes

When extensive changes have been made to a schedule, the editors include a revision note explaining the changes. As we have seen, DDC 20 introduced a completely revised, Phoenix schedule for music. A revision note is presented at the beginning of the 780 Music class. It states in part:

This schedule is new and has been prepared with little or no reference to previous editions. Most numbers have been reused with new meanings.

A comparative table giving both old and new numbers for a substantial list of topics and equivalence tables showing the numbers in the old and new schedules appear in Volume 1 in this edition. . . .[16]

Relocation Notes

Occasionally, a topic represented by one class number will be moved to another area of the schedule when a new edition appears. This is particularly true in Phoenix schedules that are completely revised or rewritten. Although this was the case for the music schedule in DDC 20, few relocation notes are found, even though percussion music, which had been placed in 789, was moved to 786 (this move is not reflected in a note).

Ex.:
782.1   Dramatic vocal forms Operas

. . . .

           Stage presentations of dramatic vocal forms relocated to
           792.5

Do-Not-Use Notes

Occasionally, the schedules include class numbers in square brackets with their headings, along with a do-not-use note. The numbers are actually derived from the standard-subdivision tables or from other add tables, and are given to indicate that a special alternative number is preferred.

Ex.:
[780.19]   Psychological principles [–019 from the standard-subdivision
            table]
            Do not use; class in 781.11

See-Manual Notes

DDC 20 was the first edition of the classification to be published with the manual incorporated as part of it. Since this inclusion, now many instances in the schedules refer to specific places in the manual for fuller explanation. See-manual notes follow see-also references.

Ex.:

781.62   Folk music

Music indigenous to the cultural group in which it occurs, usually evolved through aural transmission [definition note]
See also 780.9 for music of and performed in a specific location
See Manual at 780.89 vs. 781.62

Number-Building Notes

This category of notes is covered under *Facets and Number Building* (see p. 24).

HIERARCHIES

A quick comparison with DDC 19 reveals major remodeling of the system, although the "general-to-specific" arrangement is maintained. The hierarchical nature of the system is demonstrated visually by the indentations and typography of the headings and subheadings as well as by the numeric sequencing of each class and subclass. To understand how a typical hierarchy in music works, see the following example for instrumental music fanfares (classed in DDC 20 as 784.189 24):

784–788 Instruments and their music
  784 Instruments and instrumental ensembles and their music
    .1 General principles, musical forms, instruments
      .18 Musical forms
        .189 Other instrumental forms
          .189 2 Introductory forms
            .189 24 Fanfare form

This hierarchy is an example of increasing specificity. The genus-species hierarchical relationship can be seen in these two music examples, "Handbells" (786.88485) and "Tenor recorders" (788.366):

781–788 Principles, forms, ensembles, voices, instruments
  784–788 Instruments and their music
    786 Keyboard, mechanical, electrophonic, percussion instruments
      786.8 Percussion instruments

786.88 Single idiophones
786.884 Percussed idiophones
786.884 8 Bells
786.884 85 Handbells

788 Wind instruments (Aerophones)
788.3 Flute family
788.36 Recorders
788.366 Tenor recorders

FACETS AND NUMBER BUILDING

The faceted aspect of the system reflects one of the chief principles underlying DDC, the fact that no one class is capable of covering a given subject completely. In other words, most topics have many sides or facets—for example, a book on twentieth-century German chamber music or a collection of Yiddish folk songs. Libraries may choose to be as specific as they wish by deciding how many facets to include in classifying materials—obviously, the more facets that are represented, the longer the class number will be for any given item. Small or general libraries with no specific subject specialization might not need to include the number of facets that larger or more specialized libraries require. It is also important to remember that DDC might not represent all aspects or facets of a work.

Those who have written about DDC 20 for music have commented on the faceted nature of the revised 780 schedule. Richard Wursten noted that DDC 20 created, "for the first time in the history of *DDC*, a totally faceted scheme, modeled principally on the *BCM* [*British Catalogue of Music*]."[17] The primary facets identified by the architects of DDC 20 are, for printed music and recordings, the performers ("executants," as DDC calls them), and for literature on music, the composers.[18]

Facets are displayed in DDC through the principle of number building, which is explained in the DDC 21 Manual (volume 4):

Throughout most of the schedule it is possible to show several of the elements [from the schedule] by building numbers. Where instructions to build numbers are given, the classifier can add one part of the schedule to another part, using the digits 0 or 1 to show that a new facet is being introduced. This allows the expression of all relevant facets for a recording of Spanish folk music by a guitarist or for a score for a polonaise for piano. If a library uses a schedule only for treatises [i.e., books about music] and not for scores and recordings, the need to build numbers will not be great. Combining elements can be seen in the following:

Rock and roll Christmas music	781.723166
Christmas day	781.723
Facet indicator	1^{19}
Rock and roll	66 (from 781.66)

In this example, libraries that choose not to include the "rock and roll" facet could instead stop with 781.723, "music for Christmas day." In some situations, such specificity is neither necessary nor practical. It is important to keep in mind that increasing specificity also creates divisions. Libraries with small collections might not need to divide further than Christmas music, or librarians might determine that their patrons would like all Christmas music together, whether it be the *Oxford Book of Carols* or the *Carpenters' Christmas Portrait*. It is also important to note that the term *add* as used by DDC means "to append," and not to add in the mathematical sense.

For other examples of the facet principle, look at the examples mentioned, a history of twentieth-century German chamber music and a collection of Yiddish folk songs. As noted, these topics present examples of works that have more than one facet. It is, of course, important to determine first of all which facet should take precedence, or what the base number should be. In the first situation, there are three facets that we can identify: geographic area (Germany), chronological coverage (twentieth century), and main topic (chamber music), which itself comprises a genus-species hierarchy (music-chamber music).

Works on music	780
Works on chamber music	785
Facet for Germany (from Table 2)	043
Facet for Twentieth century (from Table 1)	090 4
History of twentieth-century German chamber music	**785.00430904**

It is important to understand that there is a prescribed order for adding facets, so as to maintain consistency within the arrangement.

This order is basically highest-to-lowest within the schedule; i.e., lower numbers in the schedules appear last in the citation order: standard subdivisions fall in 780; performers or executants in 782–788; composers in 789. Creating a faceted number, therefore, requires proceeding in reverse citation order. Also, the instructions for adding numbers within each section indicate the number of zeroes to add:

785.001–.009	Standard subdivisions
.01–.09	General principles, musical forms, instruments

A note is given that instructs to follow the pattern described in 781.1–781.7.

In the second example, a collection of Yiddish folk songs, we again can identify three different facets: in addition to the main facet, the genre folk songs, we have the language, Yiddish, as well as the format, score.

General principles and musical forms	781
Traditions of music	781.6
Folk music	781.62
Language facet (Table 6)	37
Format facet (from 780.262–269)	.263
Collection of Yiddish folk songs	**781.6237263 or M781.6237**

Number Building

Although we might consider the number-building principle to be one of the chief attractions of DDC, it is important to stress that Dewey's original system was strictly enumerative (i.e., it consisted of pre-assigned, or "ready-made," numbers for every subject). The principle of number building that has become so intrinsic to DDC was actually added gradually through successive editions of the system, to accommodate the explosive growth of information throughout the twentieth century. It was influenced by and largely adapted from other schemes, such as the Universal Decimal Classification, a British system, as well as the Colon Classification system, devised by the pioneer Indian library scientist, S. R. Ranganathan (1892–1972). The DDC Manual explains the steps involved in building DDC numbers for music.

Also called *notational synthesis*, number building allows for greater specificity by adding to a base number notation from other schedules or from special tables. There are two kinds of these tables: the first category comprises the seven numbered tables that appear in volume 4 and include what are known as *standard subdivisions*, representing languages, ethnic groups, geographic areas, etc. With DDC 21, a number from the Standard Subdivisions (Table 1) can be added to any number "for a topic that equals or approximates the whole of the class without specific instructions to do so."[20] This type of number building is known as *adding without instructions*. For multiple-term headings DDC 21 includes notes, known as *standard-subdivisions are added* notes, to guide the user in deciding whether or not these headings may be added. There are a few instances when such number building is not permitted. Some specific cases in the schedules prohibit adding from the tables; also, number building from the standard subdivisions is not allowed when to do so would result in redundancy, or for topics in standing room.

One of the simplest types of number building is that in which a full number is added to a base number. For example, the DDC number for music libraries, 026.78, is constructed from the full class number for libraries, 026, and the full class number for music, 780:

026	Libraries, archives, information centers devoted to specific subjects and disciplines
780	Music
026.78	Music Libraries (note that the final zero is dropped)

Number Building upon Instruction

In addition to adding numbers from the standard subdivisions printed in volume 1 (i.e., building a number without specific instructions), there are also many entries in the DDC schedules in which numbers are extended through specific instructions. Special tables, called *add tables*, are included for these entries. Instructions are given as *add notes*, sometimes called *number-building notes*, and apply only to the particular situation in which they are found. The number that is to be extended is known as the *base number* and is the part of the number that does not vary. To see how these tables work, look at the following broad DDC class range:

> **784–788 Instruments and their music**

> Add to notation for each term identified by * as follows:
> 01–09   Standard subdivisions
> > Notation from Table 1 as modified under 780.1–780.9, e.g., performances 078
> > *See Manual at 784–788: Add table: 092*
> 1   General principles, musical forms, instruments
> 11–17   General principles
> > Add to 1 the numbers following 781 in 781.1–781.7, e.g., performance techniques 143
> > *For techniques for playing instruments, see 193*
> 18–19   Musical forms and instruments
> > Add to 1 the numbers following 784.1 in 784.18–784.19, e.g., sonata form 183, techniques for playing instruments 193[21]

For a specific application of the "add table" principle, look at the example of Chopin's nocturnes for piano:

Nineteen Nocturnes, by Frédéric Chopin
784–788	Instruments and their music
786	*Keyboard, mechanical, electrophonic, percussion instruments
786.2	*Pianos
.18	†Musical forms (†Add as instructed under 781.2–781.8 [foot note])
.189	Other instrumental forms
.18966	Nocturne form
786.218966	**Nocturnes for piano**

Notice the two separate number-building instructions. The footnote for the asterisk ("*") tells the user to add as instructed under 784–788 (i.e., for the range). The typographical device "†" refers the user to another section of the schedules and to follow the pattern that is given in the internal table there. Although this method might seem a bit confusing at first, it also is a very economical way to save space because many classification numbers require the same number-building procedures, and patterns often repeat from one section of the schedules to the next. Also, once one becomes more familiar with the various facets of the schedule and how they are constructed, it becomes much easier to assign classification numbers without having to look the number up every time. For example, in cataloging a score of organ sonatas, already knowing that the form facet for sonatas is 183 will probably save the cataloger some time in assigning the number. Once familiarity is gained with the notational synthesis system and we understand how notes are displayed in the schedules, the principle of number-building becomes relatively simple to use. The system also permits a greater ease in analyzing numbers because someone who is familiar with its various facets and the way they relate to one another might be able to identify exactly what a relatively long number represents simply by looking at it. This type of faceted system is extremely adaptable for machine-readable access; information scientists and library theorists for several years have examined ways to combine it with various controlled vocabulary and interactive information systems.

USING THE TABLES

The seven tables that comprise volume 1 serve as an integral part of DDC's system of notational synthesis. Their main purpose is to present numbers that might be added to other numbers found in or derived from the schedules in order to increase specificity. These numbers are not to be used alone and can therefore be considered as subdivisions. They reflect the fact that many disciplines are interrelated and might share common facets. To avoid undue repetition within the schedules, these common facets are therefore presented in these separate tables and thus can be used as necessary and as permitted by the rules of the DDC system.

Two basic types of tables in the DDC are: the seven tables found in volume 1, and those lists of special notation that are located within the schedules themselves (and, occasionally, also in the Tables 1–7 in volume

1). It is the first category with which we are most concerned here. These seven tables follow:[22]

TABLE	TITLE
1	Standard Subdivisions
-01	Philosophy and theory
-02	Miscellany
-03	Dictionaries, encyclopedias, concordances
-04	Special topics
-05	Serial publications
-06	Organizations and management
-07	Education, research, related topics
-08	History and description with respect to kinds of persons
-09	Historical, geographical, persons treatment
2	Geographic Areas, Historical Periods, Persons
3	Subdivisions for Individual Literatures, for Specific Literary Forms:
A.	Subdivisions for Works by or about Individual Authors
B.	Subdivisions for Works by or about More than One Author
C.	Notation to be Added Where Instructed in Table 3-B and in 808–809
4.	Subdivisions of Individual Languages
5.	Racial, Ethnic, National Groups
6.	Languages
7.	Groups of Persons

These tables deal for the most part with topical concerns: geographic area, historical period, language, ethnic group, etc., as well as literary forms. Therefore, their application to music itself is rather limited, although there are certain genres or types of music with which the subdivisions in these tables are more extensively used, for example, music of a given region or geographic area, language, or ethnic or national group.

USING THE MANUAL

In 1982, Forest Press, publisher of the *Dewey Decimal Classification and Relative Index*, issued the *Manual on the Use of the Dewey Decimal Classification: Edition 19*, prepared by John P. Comaromi and

Margaret J. Warren. This book, intended to serve as a practical guide for students and catalogers using DDC, proved quite popular. With the publication of the twentieth edition of DDC in 1989, the editors decided to incorporate the concept of a manual as part of the classification, and thus included it in volume 4 of DDC 20, following the Relative Index.[23] (It is worth noting that Comaromi has had a long association with DDC, and also served as chief editor for DDC 20.)

Adding the Manual has proved to be a very wise decision by DDC's editors. As stated, there are several places in the schedules where see-manual notes refer users to the Manual for fuller explanation of procedures or usage, and the Relative Index in DDC 21 includes references to the Manual as well. As its introductory note states, the Manual describes how DDC is used by the Library of Congress.[24] In this sense, it is comparable to the *Library of Congress Rule Interpretations*, issued to supplement *Anglo-American Cataloguing Rules*, 2nd ed. (AACR2). In addition, the Manual is extremely useful for helping to classify difficult areas and for explaining in greater detail changes and revisions from previous editions, although it is selective, not comprehensive.

The Manual is arranged in order of broad DDC class number, preceded by information on using the various tables found in volume 1. Particularly helpful are the outline maps (Table 2), which indicate DDC area numbers for various geographic regions (e.g., the map of the U.S. and Canada provides numbers for each of the U.S. states and Canadian provinces [Quebec, 714; Montana, 786, etc.]).

Three types of notes are included within the Manual:

1. Notes on problems common to more than one number
2. Notes on problems involving only one number (or a single number and its subdivisions)
3. Notes on differentiating numbers (the notes linked by "vs.")[25]

Catalogers will find the music section of the Manual quite helpful in interpreting and understanding the schedules. Although much information from the 20th edition has been maintained in DDC 21, there are some notable changes and additions. One particularly welcome inclusion in the twenty-first edition is an explanation on building numbers. Here the

Manual explains that there are four steps in building a number for a work classified in the 780s:

1. Determine the various facets of the work
2. Arrange the facets in the proper order
3. Determine whether or not the topics belonging to the facets can be indicated
4. Follow the add instructions.[26]

An example is then given on constructing the number for a book that discusses harmony in piano sonatas composed by Ludwig van Beethoven. In this case, four facets of this work are identified: harmony (the general topic), Beethoven (composer), piano (instrument), and sonata (form). In carrying out the next step, that is, arranging the facets in the correct citation order, we need to know what that order is, and DDC 21 provides it in the Manual (p. 1170). Notice that the numbers read in reverse order from highest to lowest—this is known as *retroactive notation*:

Citation Order	
Voices and instruments	782–788 [i.e., Executant]
Musical forms	781.8
Sacred music	781.7
Traditions of music	781.6
Kinds of music	781.5
Techniques of music	781.4
Composition	781.3
Elements of music	781.2
Basic principles of music	781.1
Standard subdivisions	780.1–.9[27]

(The facet for the composer is not normally a part of the classification number, except in using the 789 option for literature about music, in which all works relating to a composer are classed together.) According to the previous chart, and disregarding the "composer" aspect of the work, the order for the facets in our examples is therefore:

• Piano (Executant)
• Sonata (Form)
• Harmony (General or basic principles)

If a library chooses the 789 option to class together all works related to a composer, the arrangement would then be: Beethoven, piano, sonata, harmony.

According to the Manual's third step for building numbers, we then must decide whether the topics we have identified are permitted by the schedules to be so indicated. At this point, the instructions within the schedule come into play—if, for example, as the Manual states, "the topic is given in a class-here note or is the same or approximately the same as a number's heading, a topic from another facet can be indicated. If the topic is given in an including note, topics in other facets cannot be indicated."[28] In this case, all three of the aspects identified in the work are capable of being indicated as facets.

The final step of the process is to follow the add instructions given within the schedule. When we look in the schedule at 786.2, Pianos, we are directed to add as instructed under 784–788, which states for Musical forms and instruments to "Add to 1 the numbers following 784.1 in 784.18–784.19, e.g., sonata form 183 . . . ."[29] Therefore, the number for piano sonatas is 786.2183. Notice the add note at 784.183, Sonata forms (indicated by the typographical device "†"), which states to add as instructed under 781.2–781.8. This note directs the user to add 1 before the numbers following 781 in 781.1–7; harmony is listed at 781.25. Therefore, add 125 to 786.2183 to yield the number 786.2183125 for *Harmony in Beethoven's Piano Sonatas*. This number might seem long and unintelligible at first glance; however, those persons knowledgeable about the system will have no trouble dividing the number into its various facets and can, therefore, easily determine what it represents. If we break down this number by its facets, we have the following:

784–788	Instruments and their music
786	*Keyboard, mechanical, electrophonic, percussion instruments
786.2	*Pianos
.18	†Musical forms (†Add as instructed under 781.2–781.8 [footnote])
.183	Sonata forms
.125	From 781.25, Harmony
786.2183125	**Harmony in (Beethoven's) sonatas for piano**

Following the explanation on building music numbers in the Manual are several examples to demonstrate how the principle works, both for works about music and for scores (i.e., music itself). Following are two of these examples, one that requires the addition of a facet indicator and one that does not:

> Variations on the St. Anthony Chorale, an orchestral work by Johannes Brahms
>
> | 784.2 | Orchestra |
> |---|---|
> | 1 | Facet indicator |
> | 825 (from 784.1825) | Variations |
> | **784.21825** | **Variations on the St. Anthony Chorale** |

> Breathe on Me, Breath of God, an anthem for three-part women's choir, unaccompanied, by Benjamin Lees:
>
> | 782.6 | Choral music – women's voices |
> |---|---|
> | 265 | Anthems (from 782.265) |
> | **782.6265** | **Breathe on Me, Breath of God** |

One important change with the Phoenix schedule of DDC 20 relates to vocal music. Vocal music is one of the most complex areas of the music classification schedule because it comprises secular and sacred, accompanied and unaccompanied, solo and ensemble, and dramatic and nondramatic types of music. In addition, the schedule distinguishes between works about the music (or treatises), recordings, and scores.

The Manual includes a detailed explanation with examples and even a flow chart to help in understanding how to classify vocal music in Dewey. DDC has historically distinguished between dramatic and nondramatic vocal music—the *character* of the music, as the Manual calls it. Traditionally, DDC has classed dramatic music in 782, and nondramatic music in 783 (sacred) or 784 (secular). Edition 20 maintained these distinctions, although the main numbers have been collapsed: dramatic vocal forms are now under 782.1, and nondramatic vocal forms are in 782.2–783. Within the range 782.2–3, DDC now distinguishes between treatises or recordings on the one hand and scores on the other. The Manual explains the reason for these distinctions:

> A person interested in reading about or listening to a singer or a piece of music will usually not know the singer's vocal range or the vocal requirements of that piece of music. In contrast, a person interested in scores will know the type of voice or voices involved, e.g., a song cycle sung by a soprano, or a Mass sung by a tenor and male chorus. Therefore, treatises about and recordings of singers and nondramatic vocal forms are classed in 782.2–.4, while scores and texts are classed in 782.5–783.9.[30]

In addition to this verbal explanation, the Manual also provides a very helpful flow chart (Fig. 2-1) that demonstrates how to select the correct classification number for a vocal work.[1] Applying the flow chart the manual then gives the following examples:

Soprano arias from opera [scores]	782.1
Soprano arias not from opera [scores	783.66
Sacred songs by sopranos [recordings]	782.25
Women's soprano voice [treatise]	783.66

USING THE RELATIVE INDEX

It is sometimes said that a book is only as useful as its index. The Relative Index of DDC has been an integral and distinctive feature of the system since its inception—it is even part of the official name of the system: *Dewey Decimal Classification and Relative Index.* There is some disagreement about the usefulness of the Relative Index, however; as Chan et al. have written in their guide to DDC 21, some

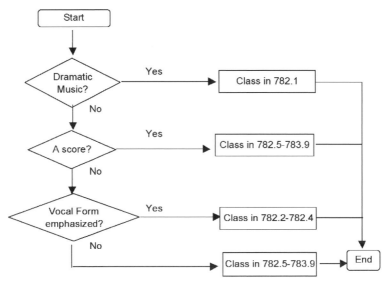

Figure 2-1   Vocal Music Flow Chart in DDC

practitioners view the index as a tool to be consulted "minimally and only in hours of difficulty" and others consider it "the door through which one must pass before entering the house of Dewey numbers."[32] Those who hold the former view might feel that classifiers should be sufficiently familiar with the schedules and how they are constructed so that consulting the index is seldom necessary. Librarians with the contrary opinion look on the index as just one more tool available to help them do their job. Most classifiers would acknowledge, regardless of their opinion of the Relative Index, that its principal benefit is to help locate the appropriate classification for works that have a complexity of facets, or those that could conceivably be classed in more than one broad discipline.

The arrangement of the index is relatively simple. Terms and concepts are presented along with their corresponding classification numbers. It is important to keep in mind always that, like the manual, the index is selective, and makes no attempt at being exhaustive. (Otherwise, there would be little need for the schedules themselves!) One does question, however, why some particular terms or concepts are included, but others are left out.

For the classification of music materials, the Relative Index's chief benefit is to class those works that are related to music, but that DDC locates in other sections of the schedules. For example, works about music libraries are classified in 026.78, music publishing in 070.5794, and music in elementary education in 372.87; treatises dealing with the music of operas are found in the music schedule at 782.1 while DDC places books on the staging of operas in 792.5, which is the drama section of the schedules.[33] These "non-music" locations for works that might have more importance to persons in the field of music than to anyone else might seem illogical to music librarians—if nothing else, it emphasizes the complexity of many topics and the interrelatedness of music with many other disciplines. The index also refers users to tables: for music history and criticism the index directs to table T3B, specifically, the subdivision 093 57. To understand more about how to apply the table, the user is then directed to the manual. In some instances, therefore, it is not unusual to have to consult all four sections of the system (the index, schedules, tables, and manual) to find the appropriate classification number for a particular work.

NOTES

1. Melvil Dewey, "Decimal Classification Beginnings," *Library Journal* 45 (Feb. 15, 1920): 152.

2. Ibid.

3. For a detailed discussion of the development and adoption of the Phoenix schedule for music, see Richard B. Wursten, comp., *In Celebration of Revised 780*, Music Library Association Technical Reports 19 (Canton, Mass.: Music Library Association, 1990).

4. [Melville Dewey]. *A Classification and Subject Index for Cataloguing and Arranging the Books and Pamphlets of a Library* (Amherst, Mass.: 1876), 20; reprinted as *Dewey Decimal Classification Centennial 1876–1976*, n.p.: Forest Press Division, Lake Placid Education Foundation, 1976, 20.

5. Melvil Dewey, *Dewey Decimal Classification and Relative Index, Volume I*, 19th ed., edited under the direction of Benjamin A. Custer (Albany, N.Y.: Forest Press, 1979), 480.

6. *Dewey Decimal Classification and Relative Index*, 20th ed. edited by John P. Comaromi (Albany, N.Y.: Forest Press, 1989), v. 4, 932.

7. An English translation of the Sachs-Hornbostel scheme, by Anthony Baines and Klaus. P. Wachsmann, was published in the *Galpin Society Journal* 14 (1961): 3–29.

8. DDC 20, v. 4, 933.

9. *Dewey Decimal Classification and Relative Index*, 21st ed. edited by Joan S. Mitchell (Albany, N.Y.: Forest Press, 1996), v. 2, ix.

10. Ibid., v. 2, x.

11. Ibid., v. 2, xviii.

12. Wursten, 34–35.

13. Lois Mai Chan, ed., *Dewey Decimal Classification: A Practical Guide*, 2d ed., rev. for DDC 21 (Albany, N.Y.: Forest Press, 1996), 25.

14. Ibid, 26.

15. Ibid., 29.

16. DDC 20, v. 3, 548.

17. Wursten, 17.

18. Ibid.

19. In DDC, the facet indicator is used to note that a different facet follows; it also is used to avoid duplication.

20. Chan, 37.

21. DDC 20, v. 3, 577.

22. It should be noted that the subdivisions listed here are further divided within the table, e.g., -092 is the specific standard subdivision for biographies, autobiographies, and other works related to persons.

23. Jeanne Osborn subsequently wrote a separate guide on using DDC 20 that was revised and edited by Comaromi: *Dewey Decimal Classification, 20th edition: A Study Manual* (Englewood, Colo.: Libraries Unlimited, 1991); also see Lois Mai Chan and others, *Dewey Decimal Classification: A Practical Guide*, 2nd ed. revised for DDC 21 (Albany, N.Y.: Forest Press, 1996).

24. DDC 21, v. 1, 1.

25. Ibid, v. 4, 902.

26. Ibid., 1170.

27. Osborn, 251.

28. DDC 21, v. 4, 1170.

29. Ibid., v. 3, 661.

30. Ibid., v. 4, 1176.

31. Ibid., 1177.

32. Chan, 71.

33. The Relative Index places spaces after every three digits within a classification number—this is done principally for ease in reading and copying, and not for truncation or abridgement of the numbers.

CHAPTER 3

Library of Congress Classification (LCC)

HISTORY AND BACKGROUND

Today, most larger academic and research institutions and many public libraries organize their materials according to the Library of Congress Classification system (LCC). Although DDC and LCC share several similarities, there are fundamental differences between the two systems as well. Melvil Dewey devised his scheme as a theoretical and unified classification of all knowledge, based on organizing principles derived from Bacon and d'Alembert. LCC, on the other hand, is founded on the concept of literary warrant, and thus is much more flexible. According to this principle, a classification system is constructed from the items particular to a given collection, and not on the universe of knowledge. The LCC system was therefore developed as a pragmatic scheme for the holdings in the Library of Congress, and as such makes no attempt to provide classification numbers for works that are not in those collections. This fact has sometimes resulted in criticism and confusion, especially because many other libraries have now adopted LCC. LCC might not as adequately represent the collections of other libraries that use it, but that has never been its intention.

Development of the present LCC system began shortly after the Library of Congress moved into its new facility, the magnificent Jefferson Building, in 1897. Ironically, it was Thomas Jefferson's own system, with some modifications, that LC had used throughout the nineteenth century. Jefferson's library, which he sold to the Congress following the burning of the original Library of Congress during the War of 1812, comprised the core of the LC collection. The arrangement Jefferson had created for his collection was, like Dewey's, based on a Baconian organization of knowledge.

In 1897, Librarian of Congress John Russell Young assigned James C. M. Hanson, Head of the Catalogue Division, and Charles Martel,

Chief Classifier, the task of developing a new system by which to organize LC's ever-expanding collections, which, by this time, had grown to nearly a million volumes. The two men had to determine whether it would be more feasible to adopt a scheme, such as DDC, that was already in existence, or, as Leo LaMontagne has written, to create one that would "profit by the experience of other large reference libraries and utilize the best features of all existing classifications."[1] After considering a number of existing systems, including DDC, Charles Ammi Cutter's Expansive Classification, and the Halle Schema of Otto Hartwig, they decided to create a new alphanumeric system partially based on that of Cutter, whose system was alphabetical. Dewey's scheme was rejected because it was "bound up in and made to fit the notation, and not the notation to fit the classification."[2] Work on devising the individual portions of the schedule was begun in 1898—class Z, Bibliography and Library Science, was the first schedule developed. The construction of each section was assigned to LC's own subject specialists, under the leadership of Martel, who oversaw the development of the schedules for the next two decades. The outline that was devised is:

A	General Works. Polygraphy
B–P	**Humanistic Disciplines and the Social Sciences**
B–BJ	Philosophy
BL–BX	Religion
C–F	History
C	Auxiliary Sciences
D	Universal and Old World
E–F	America
G	Geography. Anthropology. Folklore, etc.
H–L	Social Sciences
H	General
HA	Statistics
HB–HJ	Economics
HM–HX	Sociology
J	Political Science
K	Law
L	Education
M	Music
N	Fine Arts
P	Language and Literature

Q–V	Natural Sciences and Technology
Q	General Science
QA	Mathematics
QB–QE	Physical Sciences
QB	Astronomy
QC	Physics
QD	Chemistry
QE	Geology
QH–QR	Biological Sciences
QH	Natural History. General Biology. Cytology
QK	Botany
QL	Zoology
QM	Human Anatomy
QP	Physiology
QR	Bacteriology. Microbiology
R	Medicine
S	Agriculture
T	Technology
U	Military Science
V	Naval Science
Z	**Bibliography and Library Science**

FEATURES OF LCC

The system that Hanson and Martel devised was not radically different from most others conceived during the nineteenth century. It is relative, permitting expansion as collections grow, rather than fixing books permanently in a particular location; although it is not thoroughly hierarchical, several areas in the scheme reflect genus-species relationships. Unlike DDC, it is primarily enumerative—that is, the majority of the class numbers within each schedule are printed, and so little notational synthesis is required. Each main schedule is issued in a separate volume (some in multiple volumes), making the entire scheme, nearly fifty volumes, much larger than DDC, which now comprises four volumes. Like DDC, LCC is also available electronically.

As mentioned, LCC notation is mixed, using both letters and numerals. Main classes are represented by single Roman letters (e.g., *P* for language and literature), and double or triple letters are used for subclasses (e.g., *PS* for American literature; *PT* for German, Dutch, and

Scandinavian literature). Further subdivisions within each subclass are represented by Arabic whole numbers from 1 to 9999 (e.g., PT1891–2239 for Johann Wolfgang von Goethe). Also gaps are built into each class to permit future expansion. Although LCC's developers rejected the application of decimal numbers as an integral feature of their system, decimals have been applied as extensions to class numbers in certain areas. In addition, decimals are used in assigning work numbers (cutter numbers) for shelf location.

Because LCC's various sections were devised by authorities in their respective fields, based on literary warrant, the schedules may lack the uniformity that we find in DDC. However, each main class follows a certain general pattern. This pattern was first set forth by Martel, and is sometimes known as *Martel's Seven Points*.

These main points are:

(see Schedule p. 221)

1. General form divisions: Periodicals, Societies, Collections, Dictionaries, etc.
2. Theory. Philosophy
3. History
4. Treatises. General works
5. Law, Regulation. State Relations
6. Study and teaching
7. Special subjects and subdivisions of subjects progressing from the more general to the specific and as far as possible in logical order[3]

This original pattern has been revised to include these points:

1. Preliminary section: forms of publication and special aspects of the discipline as a whole. These include:
   a. General form subdivisions
   b. Philosophy
   c. History
   d. Biography
   e. General works
   f. Study and teaching
   Under each, geographic subdivisions may be provided.
2. Logical breakdown of the discipline into subtopics. Based on these general principles, models for subarrangement within disciplines have been established for Classes D, H, Q, and R.[4]

As mentioned, LCC was not designed for any other library, nor has LC recommended that other libraries adopt its system. Regardless, LCC maintains its popularity. This is, in part, because so many libraries have for so many years depended on the Library of Congress, especially its Cataloging Distribution Service (CDS), in all areas of cataloging, from the days when libraries purchased printed catalog cards from LC, to the almost-universal use of the Library of Congress Subject Headings (LCSH), to today's use of LC MARC cataloging and authority records, as well as Cataloger's Desktop and Classification Plus.

DEVELOPMENT OF THE MUSIC SCHEDULE

In 1902, Herbert Putnam appointed Oscar G. T. Sonneck (1873–1928), a young German-American music scholar, as chief of the Library of Congress's Music Division. Sonneck succeeded Walter Rose Whittlesey, who had served as the division's head since its establishment in 1897. The division enjoyed a number of important achievements during Sonneck's fifteen-year tenure as head. Sonneck brought the library's collections into international prominence. Early in his administration, he consolidated the collections by having all genres and formats (books on music, manuscripts, periodicals, photographs, etc.) transferred to the Music Division, thereby creating a truly unified collection. Sonneck was also chiefly responsible for the development of the Class-M schedule, which had begun under his predecessor Whittlesey. Whittlesey had organized the music collection by medium of performance, dividing vocal music into sacred and secular. Sonneck maintained this basic arrangement and expanded upon it. His original plan remains the foundation of the schedule today. As Richard Smiraglia has noted, the scheme reflects an educated view of musicology and Western art music, as understood at the turn of the twentieth century.[5] It also demonstrates very much the principle of literary warrant that serves as the underlying principle for all of LCC. The collection that existed when Sonneck became chief consisted of over 375,000 pieces of music, of both European and American origin, that had largely been acquired after 1891 through copyright deposit.[6] Sonneck also sought to increase the collection's holdings in Americana, especially early Americana imprints, as well as European music and literature.

The Class-M schedule was first published in 1904. Sonneck described the development of the schedule in the preface to the first edition:

> As a matter of course the scheme, at least so far as it concerns music proper, took a form leaning toward the classified catalogues of publishers, and somewhat different from the schemes adopted by the notable American and European libraries. But care was taken to profit by the experience of these. In its present form the scheme embodies many valuable suggestions of the Chief Classifier of the Library, Mr. Charles Martel, besides such modifications as he considered necessary in conformity with the arrangement of other classes of books in the Library.[7]

LCC:M was subsequently revised in 1917. In 1978, it was issued in a third edition, which included all additions and changes through 1977. The schedule has since been published periodically with a number of additional revisions and updates, the latest in 1998. This 1998 edition is also the first Class-M schedule to be published from a computer database. With provisional approval of the USMARC Format for Classification Data, the Library of Congress began converting its schedules to machine-readable format in 1990. Geraldine Ostrove and Harry Price of LC were responsible for the Class M conversion, which included substantial editing and indexing. The conversion to machine-readable format allows the scheme to be kept much more current and provides much greater efficiency to those who classify music materials according to LCC.

LCC:M in Electronic Form

The Library of Congress Classification is available electronically via the CD-ROM products Classification Plus and Cataloger's Desktop, two powerful and extremely useful cataloging tools that have become essential in many libraries' cataloging departments.[8] Both products, published by the Library of Congress Cataloging Distribution Service, are in a hypertext format that provides many hot links to other sections within their files, as well as to external Internet sites. They offer much faster access and eliminate the need in the earlier print versions for cross-references, tables, and indexes. One especially helpful feature is the system of links between LCC and the Library of Congress Subject Headings (LCSH). For example, searching in the LCSH database for saxophone and bass clarinet music (in that order), the user is linked directly to LC's authorized heading, Bass clarinet and saxophone music. An additional link is also provided to the appropriate class number, M288–M289 (Music for two wind instruments).

ORGANIZATION OF THE CLASS-M SCHEDULE

One of the primary differences between LCC and DDC in their treatment of music is LCC's subdivision by format: notated music is located in subclass M, but books about music are classed in ML; subclass MT is used for music education and instruction and includes scores, principally instructional methods, studies, and exercises, as well as books or treatises. (There might be some initial confusion that the letter "M" is used for the whole schedule as well as for the printed-music subdivision of the schedule.) This basic division according to format is one of the chief reasons that many libraries have decided over the years to adopt LCC or even to convert to LCC from DDC or other systems that do not distinguish between scores and books about music. Although this basic division might seem fundamental to most music librarians and music library users, there have been criticisms of this separation as being inordinately arbitrary and artificial. Scholars, for example, might prefer to have composer biographies and critical texts about a composer's music (classed by LC in ML410) arranged instead next to that composer's complete works (M3 in LCC). Shelving analytical guides to specific compositions in the same location as the compositions themselves would perhaps be more helpful to students or others interested in finding information about a specific musical work.

It has also been pointed out that in some instances, LCC classes books in M and scores in ML. An example of the former situation is that of series and collections containing volumes of both printed music and analytical texts or other types of treatises, particularly scholarly monuments (generally found in M2 in LCC) and sets such as composers' complete works (M3) that also include critical commentaries (*Kritische Berichte*) about the musical works in the edition. One good example of this situation is the new edition of the complete works of Hector Berlioz (ed. D. Kern Holoman), which also includes as a separate volume the thematic catalog of Berlioz's works.[9] As an independent publication, this book would ordinarily be classed in ML134, the classification number for individual composers' bibliographies, rather than in the M3 section with the composers' complete works. In this case, libraries must decide whether to keep the thematic catalog with the volumes of music it accompanies and to which it is bibliographically related, or place it with all of the other thematic catalogs in the library.

One option, of course, is to buy two copies and place one in each location, although most libraries do not have the luxury of purchasing multiple copies of such expensive items. Knowing the needs of their users helps librarians to determine where such items should be located. Having such decisions written in policy and procedure manuals also facilitates the process and ensures greater consistency in treatment of such materials.

In a converse situation, LC has opted to classify in ML scores that are either autograph manuscripts or their facsimiles (reproductions), except for those issued as editions for performance. The general rationale for this decision is that such autographs or facsimiles are of more interest to scholars than performers because, in many instances, they are difficult to read for performance. Librarians and others have criticized this decision, noting that it is not always simple to determine the intent of the publisher in producing such facsimiles, and some facsimiles could indeed be used for performance as well as for study.[10]

All criticisms and exceptions aside, however, the division between notated music and books about music remains useful and workable for the majority of institutions—especially modern libraries that serve a wide variety of clientele with many kinds of needs.

The flexibility and adaptability of LCC to libraries of all sizes is also an important point to emphasize. The Library of Congress's own music collections have grown to many times the size of the collection for which LCC:M was developed. The scheme is also used by many types of libraries. Yet it remains highly functional almost a century after Sonneck devised it, with a relatively minimal amount of change during the ensuing period—especially when compared with DDC, now in its twenty-first edition.

Glossary and General Guidelines

Among the many differences between LCC and DDC is that, unlike DDC with its separate, fairly detailed manual in volume 4, LCC provides limited assistance in the form of manuals or guides. Apart from the various types of notes included within the schedule itself, help is limited to the two-page "Glossary and General Guidelines" (pp. vii–viii, 1998 ed.).[11] The glossary includes the following list of ten terms commonly found in the schedule:

- Collection (including Miscellaneous, General, and Special collection)
- Continuo
- Instructive edition
- Manuscript
- Piano
- Piece
- Score
- Set
- Studies and exercises
- Teaching piece

Although this list is minimal, it is also very instructive to know exactly how LC itself uses and defines these terms. In this sense, the glossary is more like a set of scope notes. For example, under the term *Piano* is the following: "Unless specific classes are otherwise available, the term is meant to include harpsichord, clavichord, virginal, and similar keyboard instruments whose strings are plucked or struck." Similarly, the glossary instructs where certain types of materials are to be classed. As mentioned, manuscripts of compositions, for example, in the hand of the composer or arranger are not classed in subclass M (as one might expect), but rather in ML96; facsimiles or other reproductions of such manuscripts are found in ML96.5, for items "that are not meant as performance editions." We can infer from this phrase that LC considers such manifestations more as research documents than as practical performing materials. The glossary is also helpful in identifying differences between, for example, a set ("a group of compositions *published* as a single work," e.g., three sonatas published under the same opus number) and a collection, which is defined either as "an item containing compositions by two or more composers, . . . an item containing works by one composer and selected from two or more of the composer's works, . . . or an item containing one composer's works in more different forms or for a greater variety of performers than are provided for by any more specific class." It is important to know how LC distinguishes among these terms because there are, in many cases, separate class numbers for each one. These terms can also carry different meanings and can be used in different ways—even within the library community (the term *score*, for example, is used differently here than in AACR2, where its meaning is much more restricted).

Layout and Design of LCC:M

The layout of LCC is plain and straightforward. As with DDC, classification numbers are listed in the left column and the corresponding topic or verbal description of the classification is on the right. Although LC schedules are not fundamentally hierarchical, LCC:M does contain multiple levels of classification in certain areas. Each level of a hierarchy is indented from the previous level so that hierarchical relationships are clearly evident on the page. The schedule repeats the subclass (M, ML, MT) as well as the hierarchy on every page, which greatly helps the user in knowing exactly what the classification is. For example, on p. 12 of LCC:M (1998 ed.) is, continued from the previous page, violoncello and piano music:

M
            Instrumental music
             Music for two or more solo instruments
             Duets
              Piano and one other instrument
               Piano and one stringed instrument
                Piano and violoncello
                 Original compositions – Continued
230   General collections
                  Special collections. Separate works
231   Sonatas
232   Suites. Variations
233   Pieces
                   Class here separate works only
                 Arrangements
235   Collections
236   Separate works

It should be observed that parallel entries are aligned vertically and subordinate entries are indented, the result, as you can see, being a modified inverted pyramid. A heading, such as Arrangements, has no corresponding number; its two subordinate entries, Collections and Separate works, fall directly beneath it with the LCC numbers M235 and M236, respectively.

Notes and Instructions

As with DDC, each schedule within LCC includes a wide variety of notes designed to explain and guide users of the system. The following general categories of notes are found in LCC:

Scope Notes

Scope notes are usually placed directly beneath a classification number and its caption. They explain more fully how a classification number should be used and what is to be included in a class. In this sense, they are similar to class-here notes in DDC because they usually begin with the phrase "Class here . . . ":

Ex.:
M
1622   Vaudeville, music-hall songs, etc.
         Class here songs published between 1850 and 1923
         For songs published before 1850, see M1621
         For songs published after 1923, see the country of origin under
           National music, M1628–M1853

M
1473   Electronic music
         Class here music intended for performance solely by means of
           electronic media, e.g., synthesizer, pre-recorded tape, etc.
         For electronic organ, see M14.8+
         For ondes Martenot, see M175.O5
         For works for electric violin, see M40–M44.3; electric guitar,
           M125–M129, etc.
         For works for instrument(s) and/or voice(s) with electronic
           sounds, see the class for the other instrument(s) or voice(s), e.g.,
           electronic instrument and piano, M284.E4, M285.E4; quartets in-
           cluding electronic instrument(s) M485; songs with electronic in-
           strument(s) M1613.3

Explanatory See Notes

The notes printed below the scope notes in the previous two examples (the notes that begin with "For . . . ") are all explanatory see notes. They frequently follow scope notes. These types of notes, formerly called *prefer notes*, are used for topics that logically fall in more than one place; they direct the user to the location in LCC, where the concept or topic is classed.

Confer [Cf.] Notes

Confer notes, abbreviated *Cf.,* refer the classifier to another similar class number that provides more information about how the number should be applied. This type of note, therefore, saves space and eliminates the need for duplicating information. For example, arrangements for solo piano of operatic transcriptions, potpourris, etc., are classed in M39, but those for piano four-hands are located in M212. The confer note in M212 refers the user to the scope note in M39 because the same information applies to both solo and duet potpourris.

Ex.:
M
212   Potpourris, etc. and single transcriptions or excerpts
            Cf. M39, Potpourris, medleys, etc., for solo piano
            For detached overtures, see M209

[and]

M
39   Potpourris. Medleys
            Including orchestra potpourris, etc., arranged for piano two hands
            For works with title "Theme and variations," "Variations on ...,"
                etc., see M27

See Notes

See notes direct the user from a number that is not used to a number that is used instead. Occasionally, topics in LCC are relocated; these relocations are indicated by placing the number in parentheses and providing a see note that directs the user to the new location. LCC also notates numbers in parentheses for topics users might expect to find in a given location, but that are located elsewhere. These are infrequently found in Class M. The following example is for critical treatises on the literary works of the composer Richard Wagner, which LCC has chosen to class in literature (PT), rather than music.

Ex.:
ML
(410.W18)   Literary works [Richard Wagner]
             See PT2551.W36

Including Notes

Including notes in LCC are similar to those used by DDC, although LC does not really adhere to the concept of standing room in its system. These notes simply offer examples of the types of topics for which the caption of the topic refers. Several examples of including notes are in the Class-M schedule.

Ex.:
M
1003   Suites. Variations [for orchestra]
        Including separately published suites from operas, ballets, etc.

M
1680   Popular music [under Secular national vocal music for North and South America]
        Including music published in the United States in Spanish for distribution to other countries

Divided-Like Notes

The third edition and earlier editions of LCC frequently used divided-like notes to indicate when a group of numbers is subdivided like another group of numbers in the schedules. This category of note has been replaced in many sections of the schedules with instructions to use tables, and, in some instances, these notes have been replaced by enumeration. In the Class-M schedule, a similar note, a "subarranged-like" note (often as a footnote), was frequently used in what is known as a *pattern subdivision*. This was another method LCC used to save space when similar topics are treated in the same way. For example, if we consult the schedule in the third edition for works for solo piano with orchestra (M1010–1011), the schedule shows us that these two numbers are arranged or subdivided like the numbers for solo organ with orchestra:

Ex.

M

1010–1011   Piano [followed   by   a   footnote: Subarranged   like
             M1005–1006]

[and]

M	Organ
1005	Scores
	Class here full and reduced scores
	Including arrangements for reduced orchestra
.5	Cadenzas. By composer of concerto, A–Z. Assign a second
	Cutter for composer of cadenza
1006	Solo(s) with piano

As illustrated, M1010 is the classification number for a piano concerto in full score, but M1011 is used for orchestral reductions, etc. This example also illustrates the use of scope notes and including notes, as well as special instructions on how treat cadenzas.

THE THREE SUBCLASSES OF LCC:M: M, ML, MT

As observed, LCC subdivides the music schedule into three separate subclasses: M for music (notated or recorded), ML for literature about music (in all bibliographic manifestions), and MT for music instruction and study (which can also include notated music as well as treatises about music). As Richard Smiraglia has noted, "the bibliographic control of music books is no different than that of other kinds of textual materials."[12] Therefore, most of our attention here is paid to the M subclass; the

ML and MT subclasses are covered in less detail, with emphasis on problematic areas and concerns that are particular to these areas.

Subclass M

Libraries have a number of different ways of organizing their music collections (both notated music—i.e., scores—and sound recordings). Arrangement might be by composer (a simple and logical method if a collection is small), by genre, instrument, or a combination of any or all of these. LCC, like Dewey, has chosen medium of performance as its fundamental means of classification.[13] And as with DDC, LCC's chief division is vocal–instrumental (unlike DDC, however, instrumental music comes first in LCC:M). Within the broader arrangement by medium are subcategories for size of performing group, style or genre of music (e.g., jazz, symphony, or opera), and, in some cases, form of composition (sonatas, suites, variations, etc.).[14]

Although LCC:M functions primarily as a system for shelf arrangement, the subclass M of the schedule also served a second purpose at the Library of Congress for several years as a classified catalog. From 1943 until it closed the card catalog in 1981, LC used this system, rather than the Library of Congress Subject Headings, for subject access to its score collections.

A brief overview of the outline of LCC:M in comparison with DDC demonstrates immediately the principle of literary warrant on which the system is based. It also provides a "snapshot" of the types of musical works in LC's collections and how LC has chosen to organize them. For example, the very first range of numbers in subclass M, M1.A1–1.A15 (Music printed or copied in manuscript in the United States or the Colonies before 1860), illustrates the fact of Oscar Sonneck's interest in and desire to acquire early American music imprints and manuscripts and the importance LC has given these works. Other class numbers, such as M1360, Mandolin orchestras, and M1362, Accordion bands, reflect the enormous popularity of these types of ensembles at the turn of the twentieth century when the class was being developed, based no doubt on the fact that LC was acquiring large numbers of these items as copyright deposits and therefore needed separate class numbers for them. Conversely, electronic music (M1473) has only one class number, a clear inadequacy that demonstrates the lack of accommodation for the many different forms and types of electronic music that currently exist.

No doubt, many other examples could be cited to show LCC's idiosyncrasies, many of which can be identified through a brief perusal of the outline of the following schedule. LCC is largely enumerative and, on first glance, few areas within it might seem to display any obvious logical plan or appear immediately intuitive. Upon further inspection, however, certain patterns do emerge. For example, within each section throughout subclass M, the general arrangement is:

Miscellaneous collections
Original compositions
  Collections
  Separate works
Arrangements
  Collections
  Separate works

Knowing this basic pattern helps experienced catalogers locate the appropriate classification for an item much more easily. Therefore, this pattern helps to expedite the cataloging process because we find it repeated throughout the M subclass. In several places, LCC:M uses a shorthand method for this basic arrangement because the pattern is repeated so frequently. In the 1998 edition, the arrangement is located in a table (Table M2) at the end of the schedule, with a parenthetical reference within the schedule that instructs the user to refer to this table. In the previous editions, LCC instead used a footnote stating "Subarranged like . . ."; this note referred the user to another area in the schedule that followed the same arrangement. For example:

M	
15–19	Harmonium (Reed organ)
15	Miscellaneous collections
	Original compositions
16	Collections
17	Separate works
	Arrangements
18	Collections
19	Separate works

. . . .

M
40–44   Violin[1]
[footnote: [1]Subarranged like M15–19]

and

M

       Piano and bassoon
          Class here original compositions and arrangements
253   Collections
254   Separate works

. . . .

M
260-261   Piano and trumpet or cornet[2]
[footnote: [2]Subarranged like M253–254]

Solo Instrumental Music

LCC uses the term "solo" literally, meaning music for only one instrument. Instrumental solos in the conventional sense (i.e., those compositions with piano accompaniment) are classed as chamber music. This is another feature of LCC:M that some people might fault because unaccompanied instrumental solos are thereby separated from instrumental solos with piano accompaniment. (Many works for most instruments are in this second category, of course.)

Music for solo instruments throughout the schedule is found in this order:

Organ
Piano
String
Wind
Plucked (or plectral)
Percussion and other instruments (including accordion, bagpipe, and concertina)

Within the section for each instrument, the classification follows the original composition–arrangement pattern as outlined previously. For organ music and piano music, there are, in addition, separate class numbers for form of composition (one of the few instances in which musical form is considered in the classification), as well as other special types of music. There is a much greater level of specificity in these two categories than in any other solo category; again, because of the concept of literary warrant and the large numbers of these types of materials in its collections, LC has chosen to divide organ and piano music into much more specific sections than we find for other types of solo repertoire. The following is the basic outline for organ music. Notice that, in this case, LCC has even elected to provide separate class numbers for liturgical music composed for special seasons of the Christian church year:

M		
	Solo instruments	
		Organ
6		Miscellaneous collections
		Original compositions
7		General collections
		Special collections. Separate works
8		Sonatas
8.5		Symphonies
9		Suites. Variations
10		Fugues with or without preludes
11		Pieces
11.2		Pedal pieces
		Arrangements
12		Collections
13		Separate works
		Organ books
14.3		Liturgical music
14.4.A–Z		Special seasons and occasions

[Following is the list of class numbers with special cutter numbers for individual seasons. Instructions on cuttering of this type is discussed in a separate section]

Although this plan might appear straightforward and simple, there are certain problems that arise in its application. One of these difficulties is in distinguishing between collections (M7) and separate works (specifically, pieces, M11) that might contain more than one section or movement, but that are not suites or sonatas. It is important here to keep in mind the distinction LCC makes between a collection and a set—the scope notes for M7 and M11 refer the user to the Glossary and General Guidelines for the definition of Special collection and Piece, respectively, but no provision is made here for a group of works published together (a set, as defined in the Glossary). Therefore, a lack of consistency might arise (indeed, has arisen) in trying to determine whether a multimovement work or a set of pieces with one opus number is classed as M7, M9 (suites), or M11. For example, within LC's own catalog is Johannes Brahms's chorale preludes, op. 122, classed both both in M7 and M11. A similar problem arises with respect to the classification numbers for form, sonata (M8), suite (M9), fugue (M10), etc. Although the majority of these works are identified in their titles, we occasionally find works that bear some distinctive title, but that are, in fact, composed in one of these specific forms, without any indication of such in their title. These dilemmas raise a number of fundamental questions: how much knowledge of music should be required of those who catalog music and how much time should be expended in trying to determine the actual form of a work?

The problems identified with respect to organ music also apply in large measure to piano music. Because of the piano's widespread popularity and its versatility, there is probably more music for piano in the collections of the Library of Congress, and most other libraries, than for any other single instrument. As a result, LCC has provided a very detailed level of specificity for various forms and types of piano music (including some classes, such as Civil War music, that most other libraries will not need):

M	
	Solo instruments
	Piano
20	Miscellaneous collections
	Collections relating to the Civil War
20.C58	General
20.C59	Union
20.C61	Confederate
20.E7	Collections relating to World War I
	Original compositions
	General collections
21	Two or more composers
22	One composer

	Special collections. Separate works
23	Sonatas
24	Suites
25	Pieces
25.2	Double keyboard, Janko keyboard, etc.
25.3	Two pianos, one performer
	Piano, 1 hand
26	Left hand
26.2	Right hand
27	Variations
28	Marches
	Dances
30	General
31	Two-rhythm (polka, etc.)
32	Three-rhythm (waltz, etc.)
	Arrangements
32.8	Collections
	Operas, oratorios, cantatas, etc.
33	Complete works
33.5	Excerpts
34	Transcriptions, paraphrases (generally for concert purposes) of operas, oratorios, cantatas, excerpts, etc.)
	Orchestral music. Band music
35	Complete works
35.5	Excerpts
	Concertos, etc.
37	Complete works
37.5	Excerpts
38	Chamber music, part-songs, and music for one instrument
38.2	Works for double keyboard, Janko keyboard, Solovox, etc.
38.3	Simplified editions of piano music for two hands
38.5	Songs
39	Potpourris. Medleys
39.5	Works for two pianos, one performer
39.6	Works for piano, 1 hand

LCC's manner of indentation is important here; in finding the classification number for concertos, for example, it could be very easy to mistake M37 as the number for piano concertos, without realizing that this number is reserved for piano *arrangements* of concertos, unless you notice that this heading for Concertos falls within the hierarchy for arrangements. Also, the scope note (not included in this outline) states: "Class here concertos arranged for one piano (solos(s) and accompaniment)." It says further that, for cases in which only the accompaniment is transcribed for piano, the appropriate class number for solo(s) with piano should be used (i.e., M1011). LCC's use of the decimal in order to insert classes is also very evident here. In these situations, the number with the decimal does not *necessarily* have any hierarchical relationship with the number it follows—again, it all depends on whether or not the headings are indented. For example, arrangements for double keyboard (etc.) (M38.2) follow directly under M38, arrangements for chamber music (etc.), but they are not specific types of chamber music arrangements. Under the heading for arrangements for operas, oratorios, cantatas, etc., however, are complete works (M33) and excerpts (M33.5), both of which are subsets of the heading that precedes them. In this case, the two subheadings are indented.

Class numbers for other solo instruments, in contrast with the degree of specificity we find for piano and organ music, are fairly simple. Most standard orchestral instruments (violin, flute, trumpet, etc.) are listed with a five-digit range and a corresponding "(Table 2)" parenthetical note, indicating that they are all subdivided according to the standard original composition–arrangement pattern as outlined in Table 2 in the appendix. For example:

M
　　　　Solo instruments
　　　　Wind instruments
65–69　　Oboe (Table 2)
. . . .

M2   TABLE OF ORIGINAL WORKS AND ARRANGEMENTS   M2

Assign the five numbers in the span as follows:
1　Miscellaneous collections
　　Original compositions
2　　Collections
3　　Separate works
　　Arrangements
4　　Collections
5　Separate works

If we expand the range for oboe and piano music according to Table 2, we have this arrangement:

M

    Solo instruments
      Wind instruments
        Oboe
65   Miscellaneous collections
          Original compositions
66   Collections
67   Separate works
          Arrangements
68   Collections
69   Separate works

Classification numbers for "nonstandard" instruments are even less complex. Within each broad category (string, wind, plucked, and percussion instruments) and following the standard instruments in those divisions, is the category "Other, A–Z." In these places, LCC has assigned a single classification number that is then cuttered according to the name of the instrument. For example, music for the erh hu (a Chinese stringed instrument) is classified M59.E7, but viola da gamba music is at M59.V54; music for flügelhorn (a brass trumpet-like instrument) is classified M110.F53, but music for the piccolo is at M110.P5; and ukulele music is at M142.U5, whereas that for the sitar is located at M142.S5. Unlike the more standard instruments discussed above, no provisions are made for distinguishing among original compositions and arrangements, etc. The advantage of using this cuttering system lies in its expandability as LC adds classification numbers for new instruments to the schedule. (Other libraries, of course, frequently adapt the system freely to their own special needs, whether or not LCC reflects such additions.)

Instrumental Chamber Music

Chamber music here is defined as music for two or more solo instruments, up to nine instruments. The helpful mnemonic pattern that has been devised for Class M includes duets (mostly) in the M200s, trios in the M300s, etc., up to nonets in the M900s. The only anomaly is at the beginning of the chamber music section, which starts with collections of two or more different combinations of instruments at M177–179, followed by organ duets at M180. Music for two performers at one organ, as well as music for piano, three or more hands, is also classed as chamber music, even though these works are performed on one instrument. As with solo piano literature, LC has provided greater-than-usual specificity in a few sections, such as that for piano, four hands (i.e., two performers at one piano). Here are separate class numbers for sonatas and suites as well as transcriptions of operas, oratorios, and orchestral music. Again, because of the popularity of these works, LC's collections include a large number of piano duets.

As with duets, music for other instruments follows the ranges for organ and piano within each section (trios, quartets, etc.). Music with piano accompaniment comes first, similar to that for solo instruments:

Piano and string instrument(s)
    Violin
    Viola
    Violoncello
    Double bass
Piano and wind instrument(s)
Piano and plucked instrument(s)
Piano and other combinations   [including percussion]

Following music with piano in each section, this same pattern is repeated (i.e., strings, winds, plucked, percussion). To understand better how this order works, take a closer look at the example of quartets, which follows this basic outline:

Piano and three stringed instruments
    Piano, violin, viola, violoncello
    Piano, and three violins
    Piano and other combinations
Piano and three wind instruments (Table M2)
Piano and three stringed and wind instruments (Table M2)
Piano and three plucked instruments (Table M2)
Piano and three stringed and plucked instruments
Piano and three wind and plucked instruments
Piano and three stringed, wind and plucked instruments
Piano and other combinations
Stringed instruments
    Two violins, viola, violoncello [standard string quartet]

Four violins
Other combinations
Wind instruments
Woodwinds only
Brasses only
Stringed and wind instruments (Table M2)
Plucked instruments (Table M2)
Stringed and plucked instruments (Table M2)
Wind and plucked instruments (Table M2)
Stringed, wind, and plucked instruments (Table M2)
Other combinations of specified instruments
Unspecified instruments [and] combinations of specified and unspecified instruments

As with solo instruments, the schedule includes a note referring the user to Table M2 for the standard pattern of original compositions–arrangements. This same basic plan is repeated for the remainder of the chamber music section.

Many people have complained about LCC's lack of specificity and consistency, which is especially evident in the chamber music section. Because LCSH, in many instances, provides much greater specificity, we might find the lack of specificity here especially unhelpful. For example, LCC makes no distinctions among wind instruments other than for brass and woodwinds. Thus, all combinations of four woodwind instruments are placed in M457.2. The same situation occurs for combinations of four brass instruments, all of which are placed in M457.4, regardless of specific instrumentation. LCSH, on the other hand, maintains complete specificity throughout so that headings for brass quartets are delineated precisely by instrumentation. To be fair, providing separate numbers for every combination of instruments would probably result in an extremely unwieldy schedule and would also run counter to LC's basic principle of literary warrant because relatively few, if any, works are written for many combinations of instruments.

Classifying Chamber Music with Continuo, and Other Early Music

With a bit of practice, finding the appropriate classification for a chamber work is relatively simple and straightforward. This is especially true for most compositions written between 1750 and the middle nineteenth century, the "common practice" period in music history. Classifying chamber music from earlier eras, however, can be problematic. Much Baroque music, for example, includes an accompaniment for continuo. The continuo commonly consists of a bass instrument, such as a viola da gamba, bass viol, or bassoon, as well an instrument that can provide chordal support, most often a keyboard instrument (harpsichord or organ), or sometimes a lute or harp. Frequently, the continuo part as printed includes only a bass line, sometimes with numbers or figures written beneath indicating to the performers which chords to play, a kind of music shorthand. A Baroque sonata for one solo instrument and continuo, for example, might appear to be for two players, but in reality three players are required to perform it. Fortunately, the LCC Glossary and General Guidelines provides help in this instance. It instructs us, for classification purposes, to consider the continuo as if for one, rather than two performers. Therefore, a Baroque sonata for violin and continuo will be classed together with sonatas for violin and piano, in M219, regardless of the fact that three players may be involved. The same principle applies to trio sonatas (the most common genre of instrumental chamber music during the Baroque period), which are classified with other trios, despite the fact that these works require four players for faithful performance.

To collocate early music within the schedule, LCC does provide a separate class number, M990, for early music (i.e., medieval, Renaissance, or Baroque music). This is the last number in the instrumental chamber-music section. According to the scope note for the classification, M990 is to be used "for instruments of the 18th century and earlier that are generally not used in the modern symphony orchestra, including viol, viola d'amore, crumhorn, recorder, etc." We also find the instruction to "class here works for two or more such instruments, specified or unspecified, with or without organ or piano (continuo)." A number of exceptions are listed as *see* notes: music for one instrument and organ (continuo) is classed in M182+; recorder music of the Baroque and later periods is classed in the appropriate section for wind chamber music (M355–M359, M455–M459, etc.); music for ensembles of early instruments with other instruments falls in the appropriate class elsewhere in the chamber music section; and music for one instrument and piano as continuo is treated in the appropriate section within duets.

At first glance, this classification number might seem quite useful, but it can also lead to inconsistency and confusion. For example, what about all of the early music that includes scoring for "modern" instruments, such as the violin or flute? To complicate matters further, much music, especially during the Middle Ages and Renaissance, was composed without specific instruments in mind. Because LCC also provides a classification number for unspecified instruments within each subcategory of duets, trios, quartets, etc., the decision has to be made, therefore, whether to classify these types of works in M990 or with the appropriate "unspecified instruments" category. Take, for example, Francesco Bendusi's *Opera nova di balli* of 1553, a collection of dance music for four unspecified instruments. According to the editorial suggestion for performance, these works can be played by rebecs or viols TrTTB; cornetto and three sackbuts; recorders ATTB or SATB; or crumhorns. Thus, we have the option of classing this work in M990, with other early music, or in the classification for four unspecified instruments, M486. This work in OCLC WorldCat has received the class number M990, placing it with all early music that fits LCC's criteria. Conversely, we find in WorldCat (and classed by LC) Giovanni Antonio Cangiasi's *Scherzi forastieri: per suonare a quattro voci* (i.e., four instruments) composed in 1614. It has received the class number M486, music for four unspecified instruments. There are justifications for each number. An advantage of the latter is that it provides greater access for users who are only looking for music for four players, unlike the M990 class number, which places all early music together, regardless of instrumentation.[15] However, someone looking for early music within M486 will also find such works as Robert Ashley's *In memoriam Esteban Gómez*, an aleatory piece for four unspecified players that is composed in graphic notation, clearly not early music!

Instrumental Music for Larger Ensembles and Other Instrumental Music

LCC:M places instrumental music for larger ensembles (i.e., works with more than one performer per part), followed by other categories of instrumental music, in the following broad sequence:

M
1000–1075   Orchestra (including chamber orchestra)
1100–1160   String orchestra

1200–1270	Band
1350–1366	Reduced orchestra (including dance orchestra and jazz ensembles)
1375–1420	Instrumental music for children (including solos, chamber works, and music for student band and orchestra)
1450	Dance music (for unspecified instruments)[16]
1470	Chance composition
1473	Electronic music
1480	Music with color or light apparatus
1490	Music printed before 1700 or copied in manuscript before 1700

This arrangement seems generally clear and logical—it is easy to remember that music for full or chamber orchestra is in the M1000s, string orchestra, the M1100s, and band music, the M1200s. The inclusion of the section M1375–1420, instrumental music for children, is rather puzzling, however, especially the sequences for solo instrument, which separate these works from other instrumental solos.[17]

The section begins with M1000, Miscellaneous collections. LCC organizes the subsequent class numbers for orchestral music by form/genre, including:

M	
1001	Symphonies
1002	Symphonic poems
1003	Suites. Variations
1004	Overtures

In these categories, "form" is fairly loosely defined. That is, M1001 includes many works that are descriptive in nature, or that are not necessarily composed in the four-movement form of the standard symphony. The chief criterion for inclusion here appears to be that the composer has included the word "symphony" or a derivation of that word somewhere in the title. An example is Nikolai Rimsky-Korsakov's *Antar: Suite symphonique* (also subtitled *Symphony no. 2, op. 9*). As its title suggests, this is a descriptive suite, and it could conceivably have also been placed in M1002 or M1003. The designation of the work as *Symphony no. 2* gives precedence for placing it in M1001, however. On the other hand, Rimsky-Korsakov's best-known work, *Scheherazade*, op. 35, also titled *a suite symphonique* for orchestra, is usually classed with other suites in M1003.

Although seeming ambiguities like the examples above do arise, catalogers should nonetheless rely principally on a work's title in order to determine in what category it belongs. This takes a bit of the burden off the cataloger as far as having to analyze works in depth to decide on a class number for a particular composition. As with the Rimsky-Korsakov examples, there are many inconsistencies, however. Consider a work such as Witold Lutoslawski's *Symphonic Variations*, which is classified with other variations, or Richard Strauss's *Don Quixote*, a tone poem that is also a set of variations, and is classed in M1002 with Strauss's other symphonic poems.

Although LCC does not offer much help in the previous instances, it does provide a few guidelines for other situations: for the class M1003 (Suites and variations), the scope note instructs us to include suites from operas, ballets, etc., that are separately published. So, in this class, we find Bach's four orchestral suites, BWV 1066–1069, as well Bizet's two suites of music arranged from his opera *Carmen*. For Overtures (M1004) we are informed in the scope note to include preludes, entr'actes, and overtures from operas, in addition to concert or independent overtures. Beethoven's *Prometheus* overture, op. 43, as well as the four different overtures he composed for his opera *Fidelio*, are thus all found in this class.

As mentioned, the primary criterion used by LCC for dividing music for full orchestra is by form/genre: symphonies, symphonic poems, suites or variations, and overtures. Following overtures (M1004), we now turn to the section of the schedule for solo instruments with orchestral accompaniment, including concertos (again, another form). Unlike LCSH, which distinguishes between works in concerto form and other compositions for solo instrument with orchestral accompaniment (e.g., Concertos (Piano) vs. Piano with orchestra), there is no such distinction here. Thus, Franz Liszt's three piano concertos are found together with his other work for piano and orchestra, *Totentanz*, a freely composed paraphrase of the Gregorian chant *Dies irae*.

Once again, the pattern for this section begins with collections of concertos for different solo instruments with orchestra, followed by organ, piano, strings, wind, plucked, and percussion instruments, in the same sequence as other sections of the schedule covered previously. Within the class numbers for the most common instruments is the pattern subdivision scores, cadenzas, and solo with piano, as in this example for piano:

M
1010   Scores
                    Class here full and reduced scores
                    Including arrangements for reduced orchestra
1010.5.A–Z   Cadenzas. By composer of concerto, A–Z[18]
1011   Solo(s) with piano

This arrangement places all full scores of concertos and similar works together, thereby collocating all of the cadenzas and the piano reductions of accompaniments in separate sections. The instruction to cutter the cadenza by composer, A–Z, is included because, in many works, especially pre-Romantic concertos, cadenzas were not written out by the composer, but were left for the performer (usually the composer himself) to improvise. Consequently, noted performers or other composers have composed separate cadenzas to be interpolated into these works. The note, therefore, is intended to ensure that all of the cadenzas for a given concerto (or for a given composer's concertos) are arranged together, rather than being separated, which would be the case were we to follow standard practice, cuttering a work by the name of the person responsible for its creation. To see an example, the Library of Congress catalog includes these three separately published cadenzas for Mozart's Piano Concerto in C major, K. 503:

M1010.5.M8 K.503 B3 1980 (cadenza by Paul Badura-Skoda)
M1010.5.M8 K.503 B5 1975 (cadenza by Leonard Bernstein)
M1010.5.M8 K.503 R5 1961 (cadenza by Hans Richter-Hauser)

Following all of the compositions for solo instrument(s) with orchestra is the section for concertos for two or more different solo instruments and orchestra (M1040–M1041), such as Beethoven's triple concerto for violin, cello, piano, and orchestra, op. 56, or Bach's *Brandenburg Concertos*; and M1042, concertos for orchestra (Béla Bartók's Concerto for Orchestra is the most famous example in this category).

Heretofore, the main organization for orchestral music in LCC has been by genre or form—symphonies, symphonic poems, suite and variations, overtures, and concertos and related works. Of course, many works for orchestra are freely composed or do not otherwise fall into one of these categories. These types of works are classified as the subcategory Pieces, which has the following divisions:

M	
	Pieces
1045	General
1046	Marches
	Dances
1047	General
1048	Two-rhythm (polka, etc.)
1049	Three-rhythm (waltz, etc.)

The class numbers for string orchestra (M1100s) and for band (M1200s) generally follow the same arrangement as that for orchestral music.

Music for Reduced Orchestra, Dance Orchestra, and Jazz, Etc.

This general area consists of popular instrumental music for various types of ensembles in the following sequence:

M	
1350–1353	Reduced orchestra
1356–1356.2	Dance orchestra and instrumental ensembles
1360	Mandolin and similar orchestras of plucked instruments
1362	Accordion band
1363	Steel band
1365	Minstrel music
1366	Jazz ensembles

According to the explanatory note, LCC includes as part of the classification for reduced orchestra music (M1350–1353) only those works that were "copyrighted and received prior to July 1, 1944"; music received after this date is classified at M1356+, which is the range of numbers for dance orchestra.[19] This cutoff date seems rather arbitrary. An additional note explains that this class comprises works for salon orchestra, music hall music, etc., "in which the piano is generally the leading instrument." It includes original compositions as well as arrangements of pre-existing works.

It is sometimes difficult to distinguish between music for dance orchestra and that for jazz ensembles because the two genres are often very similar. Much jazz, especially during the "Big Band" period of the late 1930s and early 1940s, was performed by dance orchestras, but other dance-orchestra music is clearly not jazz. The chief criterion in determining between M1350 (Reduced orchestra), M1356 (Dance orchestra), and M1366 (Jazz ensembles), therefore, should be whether the work could be considered jazz. The simple flow chart in Fig. 3-1 can help in this determination.

Although LCC distinguishes between jazz ensembles and popular dance orchestras, lead sheets, common for both jazz and non-jazz dance

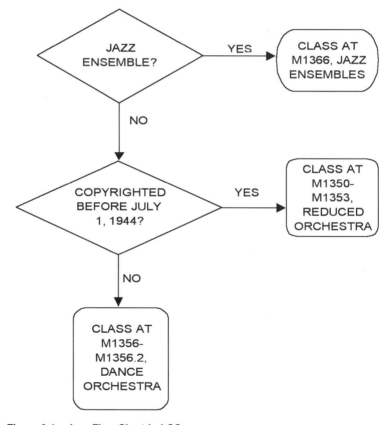

Figure 3-1   Jazz Flow Chart in LCC

orchestra music, are all classed at M1356.2. LCC separates jazz ensembles, including duets, trios, etc., classed here, from jazz solos, which are classified with other instrumental solos. That is to say that LCC does not differentiate jazz solos from other types of solos—hence, a transcription of trumpeter Miles Davis's solos in *Standards, Vol. 1* and *Bach for Trumpet or Cornet*, arranged by Michael J. Gisondi, are both classed in M88.

M1490—Early Printed or Manuscript Music

As with the classification for early chamber music, M990, class M1490 for early printed or manuscript music (pre-1700) is one of the few in LCC:M that is chronologically based. This classification was so designated in order to collocate the Library of Congress's collections of early printed music (notice, however, that early American imprints are classed at M1.A1+). Although most libraries have relatively few of these types of materials, the Library of Congress possesses some of the country's most extensive collections of early manuscripts and imprints, attracting scholars from around the world.

Although M1490 might be a useful class for bibliographers and other researchers who work with early music imprints and manuscripts, it does pose some problems. For example, it precludes any separation by genre or medium so that a collection of any size may, if treated in the standard way, be subarranged only by composer and work. Perhaps more important is the fact that there are a number of inconsistencies in its application—principally because libraries have also classed facsimiles of early imprints at this number. This fault, of course, lies not so much with the classification number itself as in the way it has been applied.

Vocal Music

When classifying vocal music (i.e., music with words to be sung), we have an additional facet to consider because text offers the dimension of topicality that is largely ignored in the instrumental-music portion of LCC:M. As with DDC, the chief differentiation in this section of LCC is between secular and sacred vocal music—thus, classification of vocal music also takes into account the function of a musical composition as well as the subject or nature of its text. Sacred music, as used here, is principally that of the Judeo-Christian tradition; LCC:M treats music of non-Western religions or Western non-European traditions with much less specificity and only in a cursory fashion. Within secular music, LCC:M makes additional distinctions between dramatic and nondramatic idioms. Further divisions include music of a national character, popular music, fraternal society songs, and songs of a number of other organizations. Perusing the schedule reveals classes for the songs of the Order of the Eastern Star, the Odd-Fellows, Knights of Pythias, Alcoholics Anonymous, the National PTA, and the United Nations Children's Fund, for example, as well as dozens of classes for topical songs ranging from "Antiques" (M1977.A65) to "Civil rights" (M1977.C47) to "Littering" (M1977.L55) to "Skydiving" (M1977.S73). All of these examples demonstrate, once again, LCC's overall guiding principle of literary warrant.

As with LC's classification of instrumental music, certain recurring patterns can be identified throughout the section for vocal music. LCC:M separates collections from separate works, and for compositions composed originally with instrumental accompaniment, it divides between full scores and vocal scores with piano or other reduced accompaniment. Patterns applying specifically to popular vocal music are covered in the section "Songs."

Following LCC's general-to-specific arrangement, the first class within Vocal music, M1495, is designated for miscellaneous collections containing both secular and sacred vocal works by multiple composers; next at M1497 are miscellaneous collections of secular vocal works by multiple composers. Dramatic music begins with operas at M1500–1509, subdivided as follows (and displaying the hierarchy in which it falls):

M

    Vocal music
     Secular vocal music
    Dramatic music
     Operas
      Including operettas, Singspiele, sacred operas, musicals, etc.[20]
      For Chinese operas, see M1805.3+
      For North Korean revolutionary operas, see M1819.3

	Scores
1500	Complete works
1501	Concert arrangements
	Vocal scores. Chorus scores
1502	Without accompaniment
	Piano accompaniment
1503	General
1503.5	Concert arrangements
1504	College operas

Excerpts

Including vocal or predominantly excerpts from works composed for specific motion picture sound tracks

Cf. M1527.2, Motion picture music excerpts

1505	Original accompaniment
	Arranged accompaniment
1506	Orchestra or other ensemble
	Piano
1507	Collections
1508	Separate works. By title
	Vocal and chorus scores without accompaniment
1508.1	Collections
1508.2	Separate works
1509	Operatic scenes

Class here independent works

For opera excerpts, see M1505+

The most commonly used class numbers within this range are M1500 (full scores), M1503 (vocal or piano-vocal scores),[21] M1507 (collections of excerpts with accompaniment reduced for piano), and M1508 (selection[s] from a single work, with piano reduction). To see how these numbers might be applied to the various manifestations of a particular composition, look at the following examples from the University of North Texas online catalog:

Opera:

Il trovatore by Giuseppe Verdi
Full score: M1500.V48 T7
Vocal score: M1503.V484 T72 1917

Choruses from Il trovatore, Nabucco, and Aida
M1507.V47 P5 1994

Miserere: from Il trovatore, duet.
M1508.V47 T765 1906

Musical Theater:

West Side Story by Leonard Bernstein
Full score: M1500.B4968 W5 1994
Vocal score: M1503.B53 W4 1959

Bernstein on Broadway
M1507.B49 M92 1981

Vocal Selections from West Side Story
M1508.B53 W4 1957

Although this arrangement is fairly straightforward and simple to comprehend, determining the distinctions between M1507 and M1508 and how LCC differentiates collections from separate works here can be problematic. Occasionally, a "collection" of arias or songs from one opera or musical is classified at M1507, with the mistaken understanding that M1508 should only be used for individual songs or arias. Although the schedule does state "Separate works" at M1508, the implication is that this term refers to the title of the whole work as well as the individual selection. In this example, a separately published song from *West Side Story* (e.g., "I Feel Pretty") would be classed together with the book of vocal selections listed here. Another potential confusion lies in determining between M1503 and M1508 for musicals, which are frequently issued as vocal scores as well as highlights or excerpts that might include a number of the best-known songs from a particular work. Rather than trying to decide whether or not a score is actually "complete" (most of them rarely are), it is best to rely on the prescribed sources of information on the item, which should clearly state that it includes only excerpts (e.g., *Vocal Selections from Annie* or *Disney Presents The Lion King: Broadway Selections*).

Another seeming anomaly in LCC:M is the decision to class incidental music and ballet music with other dramatic music in the M1500s because both of these types of works are principally nonvocal forms, and often do not include texts at all. *The New Harvard Dictionary of Music* defines incidental music as that which is "used in connection with a play." One of the most famous examples is Felix Mendelssohn-Bartholdy's *Sommernachtstraum*, composed to accompany William

Shakespeare's comedy *A Midsummer Night's Dream*. One of the movements of this work does include chorus, although many other examples of incidental music do not have any vocal parts. The same is true of ballets, which also less commonly include any sung material.

Also classed in LCC:M's section of dramatic music are works for motion pictures, radio, and television, in this order and following ballet music. Again, many works classed within these ranges are purely instrumental—especially motion picture soundtracks. Notice, however, that vocal excerpts of musical motion pictures (e.g., highlights from the film adaptation of Bernstein's *West Side Story*) are classed at M1505+, but vocal themes of radio (or television) programs are classed here with other dramatic music.

Choral Music

Music for chorus constitutes a relatively large portion of many libraries' holdings, and can range from simple unaccompanied vocal duets to large-scale works such as cantatas, oratorios, and Masses or other liturgical compositions that are scored for soloists, chorus, and orchestra. A typical choral work includes a number of facets that affect its classification, such as the nature of its text, the vocal forces involved, and the type of accompaniment it requires, if any. LCC:M, therefore, provides a high level of specificity within its choral music sections that might at first be difficult to comprehend, but it also offers some guidelines to help determine the most appropriate class number to use for any given work.

The Library of Congress's decision to separate secular from sacred vocal music means that those browsing a library's holdings for choral music will have to look in a number of different places to find all of the selections for chorus the library owns. Because many people tend to think of choral music as predominantly sacred in nature, perhaps this separation is less problematic than it might be, although it is sure to inconvenience or confuse some users. For the sake of comparison, we will discuss secular and sacred choral music classification together, even though they fall in different sections of the schedule.

Although the secular/sacred split in choral music classification might be less than helpful to some patrons, more useful, on the other hand, are the other subdivisions LCC provides for classifying works for chorus. Chief among these distinctions is that by voice type—within any given section we find music for mixed voices, followed by works for men's voices and for treble voices. Notice that LCC:M, unlike LCSH, currently uses the term *treble* rather than *women's voices*, because, in earlier centuries, churches used boys rather than women to sing the upper parts of choral works, a practice that is still observed by some choirs today. (Compositions composed expressly for children are classed in a separate section.) Within each of these sections are the usual distinctions between complete works and excerpts, and between full scores and vocal or other types of reduced scores. To compare the similarities between the classification of secular and sacred choruses for mixed voices with ensemble, see the following two examples:

M
        Vocal music
         Secular vocal music
          Choruses
           Choruses with orchestra or other ensemble
            Class here choruses with or without solo voices
           Mixed voices
           Full scores
            Orchestral accompaniment

1530	General
1530.3	With recitation
1531	Other accompaniment
	Class here works with accompaniment of string orchestra, band, other ensemble of two or more instruments, or electronic accompaniment
1532	Vocal and chorus scores without accompaniment[22]
	Vocal scores with piano accompaniment
1533	General
1533.3	With recitation
	Excerpts
1534	Original accompaniment
	Arranged accompaniment
1535	Orchestra or other ensemble
	Piano
1536	Collections
1537	Separate works

<u>and</u>

Vocal music
  Sacred vocal music
    Choruses
      Choruses with orchestra, other ensemble, or electronic accompaniment
        Class here choruses, cantatas, etc., with or without solo voices
        Cf. M2000+, Oratorios
        Cf. M2010+, Services
      Mixed voices
        Full scores
          Orchestral accompaniment

2020	General
2020.3	With recitation
2021	Other accompaniment

            Class here works with accompaniment of string orchestra, band, other ensemble of two or more instruments, or electronic accompaniment

2022	Vocal and chorus scores without accompaniment
	Vocal and chorus scores with piano or organ accompaniment
2023	General
2023.3	With recitation
	Excerpts
2025	Original accompaniment
	Arranged accompaniment
2026	Orchestra, etc.
	Piano or organ
2027	Collections
2028	Separate works

To see how each of these classifications can be applied, look at the following examples of choral works with orchestral accompaniment from the University of North Texas online catalog:

<u>Secular Choral Work:</u>

Ode for St. Cecilia's Day by George Frideric Handel (a secular cantata for solo voices (ST), four-part chorus (SATB), and orchestra)
Full score: M1530.H22 O3 1792
Vocal score: M1533.H25 O3 1900z

"What Passion Cannot Music Raise and Tell" from *Ode for St. Cecilia's Day*
Excerpt with original accompaniment: M1534.H26 O33
"The Trumpet's Loud Clangour" from *Ode for St. Cecilia's Day*
Excerpt arranged for voice, trumpet in C, keyboard, and timpani: M1535.H3
O3 1971

Notice that, if the last two examples were arranged with piano accompaniment, they would instead be classed at M1537.

Sacred Choral Work:

Jesu, der du meine Seele: Cantata no. 78 by Johann Sebastian Bach
Full score: M2020.B16 .S78 E8
Vocal score: M2023.B12 BWV78 1940

Arias from Church Cantatas: for Soprano by Johann Sebastian Bach
Collection of soprano arias from Bach cantatas with original accompaniment:
M2025.B2 M35 1949

Fünfzehn Arien, für eine Bassstimme aus Kantaten von Joh. Seb. Bach
Collection of bass arias from Bach cantatas with accompaniment arranged for
piano: M2027.B2 C36 1950z

"We Hasten, O Jesu" from Cantata no. 78 by Bach
Excerpt with accompaniment arranged for piano: M2028 .B3 BWV78 1966

As stated, the schedule for choruses in LCC:M follows the general sequence mixed–men's–treble voices. The classification ranges for the latter two categories (specifically, for men's voices and for treble voices, with accompaniment for orchestra or other ensemble) observe the patterns for mixed voices discussed previously.

Because of the long tradition of choral music as an integral element in Christian worship, LCC:M provides a fairly detailed level of classification for service and other sacred music. This is especially the case for the Roman Catholic and Anglican traditions, which are more strictly liturgical and include several different types of worship services for which composers have written music. For example, in addition to Roman Catholic settings of the Mass Ordinary (probably the most common type of setting in most library collections), there are class numbers for composers' settings of the Catholic Proper, Anglican Morning and Evening services (with or without Communion), and Communion services, as well as for music of other Protestant, Orthodox, and Jewish services.[23] We, therefore, must consider a number of additional elements when classifying these types of works. A note within the schedule states the priority to follow when determining which class number to use. See the following outline of this portion of the schedule for sacred choral music with keyboard or other solo accompaniment or without accompaniment:

M

   Vocal music
    Sacred vocal music
     Choruses
      Choruses, part-songs, etc., with accompaniment of keyboard or other solo instrument, or unaccompanied

       Class here choruses, with or without solo voices, and part-songs, anthems, motets, etc., that may be performed by either chorus or solo voices

       Class works in the following priority unless otherwise noted: 1) by type of accompaniment or unaccompanied; 2) by special text; 3) by special season or occasion; and 4) by type of chorus

       For works whose performance by solo voices is specifically indicated, see M2019.2+

2060	Collections of accompanied and unaccompanied works
	Accompaniment of keyboard instruments
2061–2068.A–Z	Collections
2072–2079.A–Z	Separate works
2080.4–2080.7	Accompaniment of instrument other than keyboard instrument

       For works for special seasons and occasions, see M2065+

       For works with special texts, see M2079.A+

	Unaccompanied
2081–2090	Collections
2092–2099.A–Z	Separate works

As the note states, LCC:M provides accommodation for choruses composed for special seasons and occasions of the church year, as well as for special texts, which are cuttered according to the list in Table M6. Here are some examples:

M
 Vocal music
 Sacred vocal music
  Choruses
   Choruses, part-songs, etc., with accompaniment of keyboard
   or other solo instrument, or unaccompanied
    Accompaniment of keyboard instrument
2079.A–Z   Special texts. By language, A–Z (Table M6)
    Including special parts of a liturgical text set as separate
    compositions

Table M6 (excerpts)

M6
  By language, A–Z
  Use an initial letter for language according to English terminology, e.g., .E1–.E99 English, .G1–.G99 German, etc. If more than
  one language is present, one of which is Latin, assign .L

Listed from Table M6 are some of the more common texts set to music:

.x11	Adeste fideles
.x16	Ave Maria
.34	De profundis; Psalm 130
.x45	Jubilate deo omnis terra, servite Domino; Psalm 100
.x6	Magnificat (My soul doth magnify)
	Class here Magnificats with or without Nunc dimittis following
.x7	Nunc dimittis (Lord now lettest Thou)
	Class here separate works only
.x74	Pater noster (Lord's prayer)
.x77	Regina Caeli
.x79	Salve Regina
.x8	Sanctus (Holy, Holy, Holy, Lord God of Hosts)
.x82	Stabat Mater dolorosa (Sadly stood the Mother weeping)
.x94	Veni Sancte Spiritus

The note instructing us to cutter by language might seem confusing at
first. It simply means, however, that the "x" in the table stands for the

language of the text (in the English form of the language)[24] and the number following applies to the particular text, so that Psalm 100 (.x45) would be cuttered thus:

English language setting:
Psalm 100: for choirs (S.A., S.A.T.B.) and bells, with optional organ, by Charles Ives
M2079.E45 I74 1975

German language setting:
Jauchzet dem Herrn, Psalm 100, by Heinrich Schütz
M2079.G45 S38 SWV36 1963

Latin language settings:
Iubilate: for mixed chorus, SATB, with piano, four hands, by David Maves
M2079.L45 M3

Jubilate Deo: a 8, by Giovanni Gabrieli (unaccompanied 8-part chorus)[25]
M2099.L45 G3

Notice that the decision to cutter by language means that the works falling in the ranges to which Table M6 applies are collocated by language, rather than by text so that settings of a particular text (and translations of the same work, in some instances) are thereby scattered. An astute patron might be able to go to, for example, .E45, .G45, and .L45 within class M2079 or M2099, and locate all of the settings of Psalm 100, but this is not too likely. The decision to cutter by language was no doubt made with the assumption that the language of a text would be the preferable collocation element, and this is perhaps true in many instances. On the other hand, this system does seem unnecessarily complicated—especially because a great majority of the texts listed in the table are from the Roman Catholic liturgy and are usually set in their original Latin. In addition, as mentioned, other ranges within this section divide and cutter by special seasons and occasions (e.g., M2078.A4 for accompanied choruses composed for use during Advent; M2088.G5 for unaccompanied works sung on Good Friday). Another result of the decision to cutter for special occasion or by special text means that composers' works are dispersed because the work number follows the first cutter in these cases.

What might be even more confusing, but what is doubtless more crucial, is trying to determine exactly when and where to classify a choral work according to its special text or season. Although the priority for determining the classification of these works is clearly stated in the notes (see the outline), the application seems to have been misinterpreted or ignored by many libraries. For example, searching in the OCLC WorldCat database for all works with texts based on Psalm 100 reveals a great deal of inconsistency, either as the result of ignorance of how the schedule is to be applied, or at least as a variation in its interpretation. Figure 3-2 should be helpful in deciding where a particular choral work is to be classed according to its text (remember that this flow chart is not comprehensive for all choral works, some of which appear outside of these numbers).

Songs

Perhaps nowhere is the history of the United States more clearly reflected than in the songs our country has produced—patriotic songs, campaign songs, religious songs; songs of love, war, and protest; and songs that chronicle important historical events or express our most intimate personal emotions. The number of songs written in America throughout the past two hundred years must surely rank somewhere in the millions. From quaint and touching parlor ballads of the mid-nineteenth century, to the classic, sophisticated gems of the "golden years" of Tin Pan Alley in the 1930s and '40s, to the myriad of different styles of song commercially available today—country, rap, alternative, rock, pop, heavy metal, and the list goes on—American popular music has come to dominate the entertainment industry worldwide. This is not to imply that other countries do not have their own rich traditions of song; they do, of course, and many of these have greatly enhanced our own country's musical styles. Nor should we omit the important contribution to Western art music that the genre of art song has made over the past two centuries as well, from composers Franz Schubert and Robert Schumann, to Hugo Wolf and Gustav Mahler, to Gabriel Fauré and Henri Duparc, to Charles Ives and Samuel Barber. These multitudes of works all echo a simple idea, that song is one of the most basic and fundamental modes of human expression.

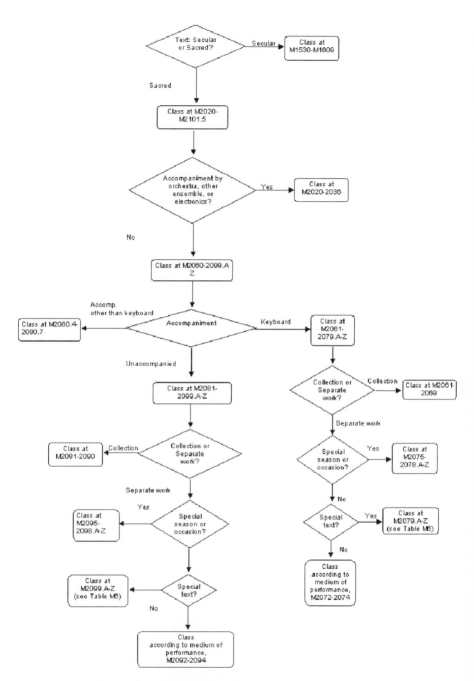

Figure 3-2   Sacred Choral Music Classification Flow Chart

The sheer volume in numbers of songs held by the Library of Congress has created a great challenge in providing bibliographical control of these materials. Part of this challenge is tied to a fact already iterated, that combining text with music adds a number of facets to consider when we classify vocal works. We have also noted that LCC's chief element in classifying a vocal composition is the sacred or secular nature of its text, a decision that facilitates classifying songs as well as choral music. As with works for chorus, both secular and sacred songs are covered here, beginning with the former.

Apart from the secular/sacred division in classification, the facets of song that are reflected in LCC:M include type of accompaniment, national origin, special occasion or function, topic of text, and bibliographic manifestation (chiefly, whether the song is published separately or as part of a collection, or with alternative forms of accompaniment). The section of the schedule for secular songs is far too extensive to be covered here in any detail. Therefore, the most commonly used classes are focused upon, as well as some of the major problems of secular song classification. The following outline of this section of the schedule will aid the discussion (the scope note under the heading "Songs" is useful in helping to determine which categories of vocal music fall under this rubric):

M
        Vocal music
         Secular vocal music
          Songs
            Including arias, solo cantatas, etc., with or without obligato chorus or refrain

1611–1618	Orchestral, etc., accompaniment
1619–1622	Piano accompaniment and unaccompanied [including piano and one other instrument]
1623–1624.8	Accompaniment of one instrument other than piano
1625–1626	Recitations with music
1627–1853	National music

            Including solo songs, part-songs, collections of texts with the tunes indicated, and instrumental arrangements
            Class here folk, national, ethnic, patriotic, political, popular music, etc.
            For composers' settings of folk music and songs, see the class for the medium of performance, e.g., choruses, M1530–M1610; songs, M1611–M1626

1900.M3–1985 Songs (part and solo) of special character
1990–1998   Secular music for children

After determining that a song is secular in nature, the next step in the classification process is deciding whether it falls under one of the headings "National music," "Songs of special character," or "Secular music for children." It is probably safe to say that most library users don't think of songs specifically in these terms. They tend, instead, to place songs in the broad categories "classical" or "art," "popular," or "folk." Although the guidelines within LCC:M are less than specific, some of the notes in this section do provide clues that may help in classification. Songs that are clearly "classical"—that is, those composed within the Western European art-music tradition (including songs by contemporary composers of all nationalities) — are classed at the beginning of the range (M1611–1624.8). This class also includes vaudeville and music-hall songs that were published before 1923. Most of the works that fall in this section are written with piano accompaniment, and are found at M1620 (for collections by one composer) and M1621 (individual works of a composer). The corresponding LC subject heading is Songs ([voice range]) with piano.[26] Songs cycles, which also enjoy popularity among singers, are classed at M1621.4. (Here it is important to know whether a group of songs was originally conceived and is published as a cycle, rather than simply collected and published together after the fact.) Vaudeville and music-hall songs published in the period 1850–1923 fall at M1622, but those published before 1850 are classed with other "art" songs at M1621.[27]

The note under the heading for national music tells us to class in this section both folk and popular music, "etc." It is also important to note that this rubric encompasses solo as well as part-songs[28], collections of song texts without music (provided that the tunes are indicated), and instrumental arrangements of national songs. This section begins to look rather like a "catch-all" category; but remember that the chief collocation element here is that of "national" character. Also notice that artistic, or composers', settings of these types of works are found instead with other art songs at M1611–1626 or with choruses at M1530–1610. For most libraries the most important note here is the one telling us to include popular music in this section. *Popular* is an ambiguous term, of course; Charles Hamm defines *popular song* as that "composed and marketed with the goal of financial gain; [and] designed to be performed by and listened to by persons of limited musical training and ability."[29] Keeping this definition in mind, it is perhaps easier to distinguish between a song by Amy Beach and one by Amy Grant or one by Benjamin Britten and one by Britney Spears; for other instances it might be more difficult to ascertain whether a song is "popular" or not. The national music section is subdivided by continent and then by country. LCC follows a general pattern throughout this section that allows for separation of popular from other types of music. In previous editions of LCC, the pattern was identified with the instruction "Subarranged like M1678–1679.2," which is the section for music of Canada. In the current edition, the pattern is retained but the sequence is printed for every country to which it applies, rather than being indicated with a footnoted instruction as in previous editions:

M	
	General
1678	Collections
1679	Separate works
	Popular music
1679.18	Collections
1679.2	Separate works

This sequence (General: Collections, Separate works; Popular music: Collections, Separate works) is found for each of the countries listed in the schedule, but the "x.18, x.2" decimal subarrangement like that listed is followed only for some of them.

This decimal subarrangement is also found for music in the U.S., as is shown in this outline:

M	
1629	General collections
1630	Separate songs (General)
	Popular music
1630.18	Collections
1630.2	Separate works

Remember that this is only a general outline. M1629 is used for general collections of U.S. songs (most commonly, folk and traditional songs); not included in the outline here are the subclasses M1629.3.A–Z for national holidays, M1629.6.A–Z for songs of geographical regions, and M1629.7.A–W, songs for individual states. These lists are quite extensive. Following popular music separate works, at M1630.3.A–Z are special songs that have their own individual class numbers ("Battle Hymn of the Republic, "Dixie," "The Star-Spangled Banner," "Home Sweet Home" are a few of these), and then an expansive section of songs on special topics (including "ethnic music"), at M1631–1677.8. To see how we might classify various types of U.S. music, look at the following examples:

General collection:
The Woody Guthrie Songbook
M1629.G88 L5

National holiday:
The Season for Singing: American Christmas Songs and Carols, compiled by John M. Langstaff
M1629.3.C5 L3

Collection by region:
Ozark Folksongs, [compiled by] Vance Randolph; edited and abridged by Norm Cohen
M1629.6.O9 1982

Collection by state:
Folk Visions & Voices: Traditional Music and Songs in North Georgia
M1629.7.G4 F64 1983[30]

Separate work (general):
"Our Flag: A New American National Song," by Pietro Marzon
M1630.M[31]

Popular music collection:
Barry Manilow Live
M1630.18 .B266

Separately published popular song:
"Misty," by Erroll Garner
M1630.2.G37 M5 1955

Special songs (by title):
"The Star-Spangled Banner," music by John Stafford Smith; harmonized by
Igor Strawinsky; words by Francis Scott Key
M1630.3.S72 S8 1941

Special songs (by topic: Democratic Party):
Red Hot Democratic Campaign Songs for 1888
M1662 .R3 1888

Ethnic music (Hispanic American):
*Hispanic Folk Music of New Mexico and the Southwest: a Self-Portrait of a
People*, by John Donald Robb
M1668.4. H52

Ethnic music (Afro-American):
"O Mary Don't You Weep: S.A.T.B. Negro Folk Song," [arr.] by R. Nathaniel
Dett
M1671.D

The whole issue of separating "ethnic music" here is fraught with
complications because many might accuse LC of marginalizing or
"ghettoizing" the music of these groups. For example, M1670–1671
is the range for Afro-American songs; the majority of the works that
LC (and most other libraries) have classed here are concert arrangements of spirituals that contradicts the note instructing us to class
composers' settings of folk music and songs with other art music
(choruses or solo songs, etc.). One might argue, therefore, that the final example should instead be classed at M1582. On the other hand,
the span M1670–1671 might be more useful for those who prefer to
browse the shelves for spirituals and other African-American songs,
"arranged" or not.

Although the subarrangement of secular songs according to country of origin might generally still be helpful to users, the decision to
include popular music here has probably outlived its usefulness because most critics would argue that current popular music cuts across
geopolitical boundaries. This all began, of course, in the 1960s with
the "British invasion" of the Beatles and other English pop groups.
Irrespective of the fact that the music of these groups has been heavily influenced by various American popular and vernacular idioms

(including, most noticeably, African-American genres), libraries have classed the music of the Beatles, Elvis Costello, Elton John, and Sting, among many other examples, at M1741.18–1741.2, the range for English popular music. This, of course, leads to confusion for library users, and the danger of inconsistency and shelf dislocation because many catalogers might not themselves know a popular entertainer's country of origin. And what about all of those performers from elsewhere who currently live and work in the U.S.? In the case of Elvis Costello, some libraries have classed his music at M1627 (international collections), which might seem safe and logical; LC has classed collections of his music both in American popular and English popular music (M1630.18 and M1741.18). Although LCSH and the LC Subject Cataloging Manual have made it fairly clear that the geographical subdivision " — United States" should not ordinarily be used for most popular music (unless the work specifically states a geographical emphasis), we are not given this opportunity in LCC:M because the main point of subdivision here is that of nationality.

Perhaps a more useful arrangement of popular music, especially for public libraries or for those institutions that have large collections of these materials, would be one according to style ("Country," "Rock," "Hip-hop," etc.), with class numbers that coordinate with LC subject headings already applied to these works. A simple method of implementing this could be to use cutters, as other sections here already do, so that country music collections could all be placed at M1630.18.C7, for example. Reclassifying existing collections is difficult, although it is not uncommon for libraries that use DDC, of course.

Songs of a "special character" follow national songs and are classed at M1977 (collections) and M1978 (separate works). The two classes are cuttered .A–Z by topic, with the list of topics (which is quite extensive) enumerated in the schedule. Although this section is separated from that of national songs, many of the topics listed have a distinctly American connection (e.g., cowboy or basketball songs). The list includes a number of cross-references that are helpful (all sports are cuttered under ".S" — golf at .S72, soccer at .S75). Some people might take offense at the fact that Girl Scout songs are cuttered under ".B6" with those for Boy Scouts, but at least a cross reference shows this.

Songs with religious texts (specifically, those of the Christian, Jewish, and Islamic faiths) are classed in the range M2102–2114.4.A–Z.

The scope note under the heading states that included here are "arias, solo cantatas, etc., with or without obligato chorus or refrain." As can be seen in the outline for this section, the chief element of collocation here, as it is for sacred choral works, is the type of accompaniment. Likewise, original compositions are distinguished from arrangements, collections from separate works, and full scores from those with reduced accompaniment.

M
        Vocal music
          Sacred vocal music
            Songs
2102–2108   Orchestral, etc. accompaniment
2110–2114.4.A–Z Accompaniment of piano, etc., and unaccompanied
                Including accompaniment of one instrument of any type and of two instruments, one of which is chordal

The flow chart for the classification of sacred choruses found in Fig. 3-2 can also apply in classifying sacred songs—specifically, those songs with piano accompaniment that also have a text falling within the "Special text" category listed in Table M6, and those composed for special seasons and occasions (classed at M2114.4.A–Z).

Hymnals, Collections of Hymns, and Liturgical Music

Because of the important role music plays in most religious practices around the world, many libraries have extensive collections of hymnals and other music related to worship. The term *hymnal* can also be applied to books of hymn texts without music (to be precise, a hymn is a text to be sung to a hymn tune). Hymnals that do not include musical notation are therefore classed in the religion section at BV1+ (this rule also applies to those books in which tune names are indicated, but that omit notated music). LCC organizes hymnals and other hymn collections first by tradition (Christian, Jewish, and other religions) and then by country (for the United States) or language (for South America and Europe). U.S. hymnals are further subarranged by denomination.

The section of LCC:M following hymns is designated for liturgy and ritual. This complex and extremely detailed area is one in which many catalogers, even those with extensive music backgrounds, may lack expertise. Having at hand a dictionary or handbook on church music is therefore helpful in dealing with these types of materials. Some recent publications include David Poultney's *Dictionary of Western Church Music* (Chicago: American Library Association, 1991) and *Worship Music: A Concise Dictionary*, edited by Edward Foley (Collegeville, Minn.: The Liturgical Press, 2000).

As the scope note at the beginning of the liturgy and ritual section states, the main criterion to consider in determining what to class here is whether the work in question is "officially prescribed." The note also tells us to class all other church music that is "composed to sacred texts for use in church services . . . as provided in the schedule." The key phrase here is "officially prescribed"; the works in this class, in other words, should be those that are issued or recognized by the governing body of the church or denomination in question. *AACR2* defines a liturgical work as one that "includes officially sanctioned or traditionally accepted texts of religious observance, books of obligatory prayers to be offered at stated times, calendars and manuals of performance of religious observances, and prayer books known as 'books of hours.'"[32] There is, of course, a rich tradition of sacred music, both choral and solo vocal, that does not fall within this rubric. The various types of works that should be classed at the appropriate place in the schedule, as the previous note instructs are covered elsewhere in this book.

This section is most applicable to the Roman Catholic, Orthodox, and Anglican traditions. The Roman Catholic and Orthodox traditions are by far the oldest in the Christian church as well as the most ritually complex. They, and the various churches in the Anglican communion, are all highly structured with prescribed rituals and music for many types of formal worship services. The range of class numbers for the Roman Catholic Church, in particular, is quite extensive, no doubt because of the proliferation of Catholic liturgical publications that the Library of Congress has acquired. This section (beginning with printed music at M2148.A–Z) is:

M

  Vocal music
   Sacred vocal music

	Liturgy and ritual
	Roman Catholic Church
	Printed music
2148.A–Z	Graduals [including Propers and Ordinaries]
2149.A–Z	Antiphonaries [i.e., music for the Divine Office]
2150–2150.4.A–Z	Special ceremonies and occasions
2151.A–Z	Liber usualis
2152–2154	[Directories, miscellaneous collections, special liturgies and rituals, non-Roman rituals, and modern schisms]

As the outline implies, several areas within this section are cuttered according to prescribed tables listed at the appropriate places within the schedule. The procedures to follow in applying these tables are like those in other similar areas with enumerated cuttered lists throughout the schedule.

Jewish liturgical music that is classed in this section (M2186–2187) includes traditional music intended for worship in the synagogue, as well as unaccompanied music for cantor, and collections containing both traditional and originally composed music. Other Jewish service music is classed at M2017.6.

As in other areas of LCC:M, sacred vocal music for children follows the other sacred vocal sections at M2190–2196. The area includes dramatic and choral works and songs (both solo and part-songs). Popular religious or devotional music is the last category in LCC:M (apart from M5000, Unidentified compositions) and is found at M2198–2199. The latest edition of LCC:M reflects the addition of contemporary Christian music to the scope note for this range, which also includes gospel, revival, and temperance songs.

Subclass ML: Literature on Music

With the tremendous growth in music scholarship over the past three decades, libraries have seen an ever-increasing demand for, and supply of, books about music. The "publish-or-perish" syndrome that pervades American academia is, in part, responsible for this boom, but the phenomenon is also evident in popular, nonspecialist music literature as well. This proliferation in music publishing creates for libraries greater and greater challenges in all functions, from collection development, to reference and public service, to cataloging and processing. The imminent demise of print has long been foretold, but the book seems to be as healthy as ever, even with the advent of the World Wide Web and other electronic media. The system Oscar Sonneck devised a century or so ago to classify music materials, separating music from books about music, still works remarkably well today, even though we have so many more books on so many more topics than Sonneck ever envisioned (although he would no doubt be happy to see the growth in American-music studies because he was a pioneer scholar in this field). Also remember that Sonneck's class M conforms closely to the principles that underlie the entire Library of Congress classification system. Richard Smiraglia has noted that all of Charles Martel's "Seven Points" of classification can be observed in LCC:M. Of these seven points, Smiraglia identifies in particular the following five in the ML subclass:

1. General form divisions
3. History. Biography
4. Treatises. General works
5. Law. Regulation. State relations
7. Subjects and subdivisions of subjects[33]

The subclass ML follows the general pattern established for other classes within LCC. In keeping with the first of Martel's points, the ML subclass begins with periodicals and serials at ML1–5 (note that treatment of periodicals varies among libraries—many do not classify them, or only class certain types, such as annuals, yearbooks, etc.), followed by other general form divisions (directories, literature on societies, etc.). This sequence can be observed in the outline of LCC:M in Appendix I.

Application of the ML subclass is fairly straightforward and simple. The entire subclass is highly enumerative. In many cases, topics and subtopics are brought out through the use of cuttering, with extensive lists of subtopics included for many subjects. Here are some representative examples:

ML
        Dictionaries. Encyclopedias
102.A–Z   By topic, A–Z
102.J3   Jazz (e.g., *New Grove Dictionary of Jazz*)
102.V4   Violin (e.g., *The Violinist's Encyclopedic Dictionary*)

Bibliography
128.A–Z   By topic, A–Z
128.S247   Saxophone (e.g., *125 ans de musique pour saxophone*)

Discography
156.4.A–Z   By topic, A–Z
156.4.R6   Rock music (e.g., *The Trouser Press Guide to '90s Rock*)
156.7.A–Z   Individual performers, A–Z [not listed]
156.7.P35   Charlie Parker (e.g., *The Dial Recordings of Charlie Parker*)

The most complicated aspects of the ML schedule deal more with applying tables, which is covered in a separate section. Still, some points should be kept in mind in regard to this portion of LCC:M:

Periodicals and Serials (ML1–5)

This range applies only for general music periodicals. Those that are more specifically about one aspect of music are classed with that particular topic. For example, *The Musical Quarterly* is classed by LC in ML1, and *7-Ball Magazine* (a Christian rock magazine) is found at ML3187.5, the class number for works about contemporary Christian music. LC classes the blues magazine *Juke Blues* at ML3520.8, the number for blues periodicals; a similar periodical, *Jazz & Blues*, however, is classed in the ML1–5 span for general periodicals (ML1.J), since it covers more than one specific topic. Journals that are the official organs of societies (e.g., *Notes: the Quarterly Journal of the Music Library Association* and the *Journal of the American Musicological Society* [*JAMS*]) are classed at ML27.U5 under national societies and organizations (ML27.A–Z, cuttered by country). Another important point to remember with periodicals is that, in keeping with Martel's "Seven Points," even those that are classed topically always come at the beginning of the appropriate section, as in the following:

ML
                Instruments
                Keyboard instruments
                Organ
549.8   Periodicals. Societies. Serials

549.9   Congresses
550   General works

Manuscripts and Facsimiles

To reiterate a point concerning the inconsistencies within LCC:M, even though the ML subclass is designated for literature about music, it does allow for the classification of notated music in some areas. Most notable among these examples is the span ML96–96.5, manuscripts of musical compositions and their facsimiles. The exceptions to this application, as stated in the notes, include those manuscripts and facsimiles of liturgical music for the Roman Catholic and Orthodox churches (classed instead of M2147 and M2156, respectively), historical collections (classed instead M2+), and those intended as performing editions (classed instead at the appropriate number in subclass M). Again, the logic behind this decision is that these materials are of greater interest to scholars than to performers because they are, in many cases, not legible enough to use for performance.

Music Librarianship, Printing, Bibliography, and Discography

Music librarianship, printing, bibliography, and discography are among those hybrid, multifaceted fields that conceivably could fall in more than one class within LCC. All of the topics named here, for example, might also fit within class Z (library science and bibliography). The creators of LCC decided instead that both music librarianship and music bibliography should be classed within ML. In fact, within class Z, the section for cataloging (Z695.1.A–Z) includes a *see* reference for music cataloging at ML111. On the other hand, the scope note at ML111 states that cataloging of sound recordings "in general" is at Z695.715. Similarly, music and law (class K) are the only two areas in LCC in which bibliographies are classed within the subject, rather than in class Z.

Biography

One of the most extensive areas within most libraries' collections of music literature is that of musicians' biographies, which LCC classes in the span ML385–429. Collective biographies are divided from works about individuals; each of these two sections is also subarranged according to the following sequence:

Composers
Performers
  Instrumentalists
   Organists
   Pianists
   Violinists, violoncellists, etc.
   Other instruments
  Singers
Conductors
Theoreticians, historians, critics, etc.
  Including librettists
  For works on writers of hymn texts, see BV
Manufacturers of instruments
Music publishers, printers, dealers
Managers and others (this category is found only under individual biography)

Of these various categories, biography of individual composers (ML410.A–Z) is by far the largest. Biography here includes, as the note indicates, historical, as well as biographical treatments of a composer's life; works that are primarily analyses of composers' music are instead classed at MT90+ (Analysis and appreciation of musical works). This split could present problems, as in the following two examples:

Bartók Chamber Music by Stephen Walsh
MT145.B25 W23 1982

Bartók's Chamber Music by János Kárpáti
ML410.B26 K413 1994

Without examining the content of these two works, the first one might seem more analytical and the second more historical in its treatment of Bartók's chamber compositions. Nonetheless, most patrons would probably prefer to see the two books together on the shelf. Also notice that ML410 includes biographies of all composers, including popular-music composers, not just composers of Western art music. As the note under performers (ML420) states, musicians who are known both as performers and composers are to be classed according to the "relative importance" of their "activity in the different fields of music." Few, if any, individuals have ever been so prodigious in so many different and disparate fields of study as Albert Schweitzer, whose contributions ranged from theology to philosophy, medicine, and music. LCC:M instructs us to classify works about Schweitzer in the class number most appropriate to the individual work (B2430.S37 for Schweitzer as philosopher, BX4827.S35 as theologian, CT1018.S45 for general biography, R722.32.S35 as medical missionary, or ML416.S33 as organist).

Like other biographies in LCC, as well as those in DDC, individual biographies in subclass ML are cuttered according to the subject of the biography, then by author. The 1998 edition of the schedule lists a few specific composers with their cutter numbers (and what an odd list it is!). This list is not proscriptive, of course, and any other composer may be included here. Of the composers listed, J. S. Bach and Ludwig van Beethoven are subdivided, as follows:

ML
          Bach, Johann Sebastian, 1685–1750
410.B1   General works
410.B13   Critical works
410.B14   Family of Johann Sebastian Bach

          Beethoven, Ludwig van, 1770–1827
410.B4   General works
410.B42   Critical works

LCC also provides the possibility for extending class numbers of individual biographies to a more detailed or specific level, particularly for those biographees who have been the subject of many works. This option, which pertains to all classifications, except classes N and P, is delineated in a table found in the Library of Congress *Subject Cataloging Manual: Shelflisting*:

x   Cutter for the biographee
.xA2   Collected works. By date
.xA25   Selected works. Selections. By date
               Including quotations

.xA3	Autobiography, diaries, etc. By date
.xA4	Letters. By date
.xA5	Speeches, essays, and lectures. By date
	Including interviews
.xA68–Z	Individual biography, interviews, and criticism.
	By main entry
	Including criticism of selected works, autobiography, quotations, letters, speeches, interviews, etc.[34]

LCC:M follows a modified version of this pattern for the composer Richard Wagner, the only composer to have a complete expansion within ML410 (ML410.W1A1–.W2). Previous editions of LCC:M included a note stating that this subarrangement may be used as a pattern for classing other biographies in ML410, "in exceptional cases with the necessary variations."[35] One reason that LCC has chosen to expand the section for classifying Wagner biographies in such great detail is because, in addition to being one of the most written-about individuals in history, Wagner himself was such a prolific writer of prose as well as musical works. Despite the extensiveness of this span, it does follow in general terms the pattern outlined above, although the individual cutters do not necessarily correspond exactly. Other major composers, J. S. Bach, Beethoven, Johannes Brahms, Frédéric Chopin, Joseph Haydn, W. A. Mozart, Franz Schubert, Robert Schumann, to name a few, are treated by LC in the same way, with the cutter ".Ax" standing for works by the composer (letters, diaries, biographical works, etc.), followed by critical works.

Instrumental and Vocal Music

Looking at the ranges for instrumental and vocal music (see Appendix I), it is fairly simple to discern that LCC:M follows the same pattern in this section as it does for subclass M: that is, works on instruments and instrumental music precede those on vocal music. Instruments fall in the same order as in subclass M (keyboard, stringed, wind, plucked, percussion, other, electronic), followed by ensembles (again, in the same order—chamber, orchestral, band), then vocal music (choral, then secular and sacred vocal). Within each, section treatment is subarranged geographically, and there is extensive application of tables throughout.

Popular Music

Unlike its treatment of popular music as a special subset within national music in subclass M, LCC:M places the literature on popular music in a separate, "second-tier" hierarchy in subclass ML, directly under history and criticism. Following periodicals, etc., and general works, this section is then subdivided geographically (America [North and South], Europe, Asia, Africa, Australia), after which comes the subcategory "Types and styles," which includes first jazz, then an alphabetical listing of other popular genres, from barbershop quartets to ragtime to techno and Western swing music.

Subclass MT: Musical Instruction and Study

The third of the three main subclasses within class M, subclass MT, is designated for the instruction and study of music. As Smiraglia notes, this subclass focuses on the second and sixth of Martel's Seven Points (theory and philosophy; and study and teaching, research, and textbooks, respectively).[36] Although the shortest of the three, subclass MT covers a much broader range of topics than we might think because it encompasses subjects of interest to those persons involved in music education at the primary and secondary levels, as well as theoretical and analytical topics and pedagogical works. Here is the general outline:

MT	
	Musical instruction and study
1–5	Theory and history of music education
5.5–7	Music theory
20–32	Special methods
40–67	Composition. Elements and techniques of music
68	Improvisation. Accompaniment. Transposition
70–74	Instrumentation and orchestration
90–146	Analysis and appreciation of musical works
170–810	Instrumental techniques[37]
820–949	Singing and vocal technique

As discussed, the MT subclass is one area in which LCC's strict division between books and music is less well defined. This can be seen in the last two categories, which can include printed music, such as studies and exercises, instructive editions, and other types of teaching pieces. Therefore, these categories of printed music are classed here, rather than in subclass M. In most cases, it is relatively simple to determine whether a work of this type should be classed in M or MT, but there are some instances in which catalogers must use their best judgment in making these decisions. The definition of *instructive edition* in the Glossary and General Guidelines is somewhat helpful here: such editions are identified as those "heavily annotated with textual instructions about how to practice and interpret various passages."[38] According to the definition, this type of work goes beyond the mere addition of fingering and other types of interpretive markings, whether those of other editors or of the composer. This definition, however, does leave room for a fair amount of subjectivity in its interpretation, and it also presents the possibility that different editions of a composer's works are located in entirely different sections of the library. One good example is Artur Schnabel's edition of the complete piano sonatas of Beethoven, originally published in 1935.[39] Many libraries follow LC's practice and class this edition at MT247 rather than M23. Libraries must decide whether the nature and amount of instructive material that Schnabel includes in his edition warrants separating it from the remainder of Beethoven's piano sonatas (and thereby facing the possibility of complaints from impatient faculty who do not take time to consult the catalog because they know exactly where all the piano music in the library is supposed to be!).

The Glossary also defines a teaching piece as one written "principally for pedagogical purposes." This definition might seem rather self-evident, but the distinction gains more meaning when considering such genre pieces as the etudes of Chopin or Debussy, both of which should be considered more as artistic creations than pedagogical works. Nonetheless, these types of works are often classed in MT, rather than in subclass M.

As in the other subclasses, within subclass MT are some patterns that repeat several times. One of the most frequent of these patterns is the one for types of instrumental techniques, which is found two ways in the latest edition: either written out or notated in a table. For most standard instruments the pattern is delineated with separate numbers for each type of work, as in this example under "Oboe" (the pattern varies slightly with some instruments):

MT
      Instrumental techniques
      Wind instruments
        Oboe
360   General works
362   Systems and methods
363   Teaching pieces
364   Instructive editions
365   Studies and exercises
366   Orchestral studies
367   Two oboes
368   Self-instructors

For other instruments in this section, the user is referred to Table M5, which includes a decimal extension for applying the sequence.

Tables and Index

One feature that is new with the 1998 edition of LCC:M is the addition of ten external tables at the end of the schedule (pp. 185–198). These include tables of frequently used patterns, as well as tables of special cutters, such as for geographical areas, special texts, etc. These tables, in part, supplant the use of patterns notated as footnotes in earlier editions. They also accommodate "hot links" in the electronic, hypertext version of the schedule, published as Classification Plus. The use of these tables in LCC offers a degree of synthesis or number building that is more usually associated with DDC.

Table M1: States and Regions of the United States

Certain sections in both the M and ML subclasses require geographical subdivision by U.S. state or region. This subdivision is assigned from the external cutter table M1. The sections that use this table include M1629.7.A–W (collections of national songs of the U.S.), M1658.A–W (separate songs about states), ML14.A–Z (U.S. directories and almanacs), and ML106.U4A–Z (state and regional bio-bibliographical dictionaries and encyclopedias). In addition, four other tables of geographic subdivisions, M4, M8, M9, and M10, also refer to this table for additional subdivision by state or region. Here are some examples of the application of this table:

> *Louisiana French Folk Songs,* by Irène Thérèse Whitfield
> M1629.7.L8 W54 1939 (.L8 for Louisiana)

> *South Carolina, the Palmetto State*, by Lily Strickland; words by Harry Russell Wilkins
> M1658.S6 S76 (.S6 for South Carolina)

> *Directory of Music Collections in the Greater NewYork Area*, by Nina Davis-Millis
> ML14.N6 D3 1983 (.N6 for New York)

> *Traditional Musicians of the Central Blue Ridge*, by Marty McGee
> ML106.U4 B66 2000[40]

Table M2: Table of Original Works and Arrangements

The sequence for original works and arrangements outlined in Table M2 is one of the most frequently applied in subclass M. Its application in classifying instrumental solo and chamber music is discussed more fully on pp. 55–56 and 59–60. The table is also used in the span M1413–1417 (instrumental trios, quartets, etc., for children).

Table M3: Table of Subdivisions for Regions (1 No.)

Table M3 is used heavily throughout the ML subclass. This is not a table of geographic subdivisions, as its title might seem to imply. It is rather a period subdivision and is applied by the addition of a one-digit decimal extension to the prescribed class numbers for which it is applicable. Here is the table (where 0 stands for the class number notated in the schedule), followed by some examples of its usage:

0	General works
0.1	Addresses, essays, lectures[41]
	By period
0.2	Early to 1700

0.3	1701–1800
0.4	1801–1900
0.5	1901–2000
0.6	2001–

Ex.:
Histoire de la musique européenne, 1850–1914, by Camille Mauclair
ML240 .M3 1914 (General work on the history of music in Europe)

Asian Music and Dance: Educational Perspectives: a collection of papers given at the Asian Music and Dance Conference in Education in Singapore, March 16–19, 1997, edited by Eugene Dairianathan
ML330.1 .A85 1997 (proceedings of a conference on Asian music; with extension 0.1 from table, for addresses, essays, lectures)

Fortepianos and Their Music: Germany, Austria, and England, 1760–1800, by Katalin Komlós
ML720.3 .K66 1995 (historical treatment of the fortepiano in eighteenth-century Europe, with extension 0.3 from table, for 1701–1800)

Ballet and Opera in the Age of Giselle, by Marian Elizabeth Smith
ML1720.4 .S65 2000 (historical treatment of nineteenth-century dramatic music in Europe, with extension 0.4 from table, for 1801-1900)

Americas, Essays on American Music and Culture, 1973–1980, by Peter Garland
ML198.5 .A43 1982 (general work on 20th-century American music —including North and South America, with extension 0.5 from table, for 1901–2000)

Table M4: Table of Subdivisions for Countries (1 No.)

Table M4 is identical to M3 with the addition of three decimal extensions to accommodate geographic subdivision:

0	General works
0.1	Addresses, essays, lectures
	By period
0.2	Early to 1700
0.3	1701–1800
0.4	1801–1900
0.5	1901–2000

0.7A–Z   By state, province, etc., A–Z
              For regions and states of the United States, see Table M1

0.8   A–Z By city, A–Z
              For works on a specific city in relation to a topic, see the topic,
              e.g., ML1711.8.P5, Opera in Philadelphia; for works on a spe-
              cific   society,   including   performing   ensembles,   see
              ML26–ML28; for works on a specific festival, including per-
              formance festivals, see ML36–ML38
0.9   Other

Table M4 is used much more frequently than M3. Notice that the table
permits subdivision either by period (for works on the U.S. as a whole)
or by individual state or city, although there is no accommodation for
both facets. Here is how Table M4 is applied in the class number
ML200, historical and critical works on music in the United States:

America's Musical Life: a History, by Richard Crawford
ML200 .C69 2001 (General work on the history of music in the U.S.)

*Vistas of American Music: Essays and Compositions in Honor of William K.
Kearns*, ed. by Susan L. Porter and John Graziano
ML200.1 .V57 1999 (collection of essays, with extension 0.1 from table, for
addresses, essays, lectures)

The Music of the Pilgrims, by Waldo Selden Pratt
ML200.2 .P7 1971 (historical treatment of early American music, with extension 0.2 from table, for early works to 1700)

Early Concert-Life in America (1731–1800), by O. G. Sonneck
ML200.3 .S6 1907 (history of eighteenth-century American music, with extension 0.3 from table, for 1701–1800)

*Music in the Cultured Generation: a Social History of Music in America,
1870–1900*, by Joseph A. Mussulman
ML200.4 .M9 (history of late-nineteenth-century American music, with extension 0.4 from table, for 1801–1900)

All American Music: Composition in the Late Twentieth Century, by John
Rockwell
ML200.5 .R6 1983 (discussion of the current state of music composition in
the U.S., with extension 0.5 from table, for 1901–2000)

Hawaiian Music and Musicians: an Illustrated History, ed. by George S. Kanahele
ML200.7.H4 H45 (history of music in Hawaii, with extension 0.7 from table (by state), and with cutter .H4 from Table M1 for Hawaii)

Musical Gumbo: the Music of New Orleans, by Grace Lichtenstein and Laura Dankner
ML200.8.N48 L5 1993 (history of music in New Orleans, with extension 0.8 from table (by city), and with cutter .N48 for New Orleans)

The Saint Olaf Choir: a Narrative, by Joseph M. Shaw
ML200.9.S2 S53 1997 (with extension 0.9 from table, for other types of works not listed elsewhere in the table)

Table M5: Table of Subdivisions for Instrumental Instruction and Study

Like Table M2, for original works and arrangements, Table M5 is a sequence of subdivisions by type of material, rather than by historical or geographical treatment. The discussion of instrumental instruction and study in subclass MT (p. 98+) focused on the pervading pattern for these various types of works as exemplified under the heading for oboe; this span or similar ones is located throughout subclass MT for most standard instruments. For less-common instruments, we are instead referred in the schedule to Table M5, which includes a list of decimal extensions that may be added to the applicable class number. As in the previous tables, the *0* represents the class number in the schedule:

0	General works
0.2	Systems and methods
0.3	Studies and exercises
0.4	Orchestral studies
0.5	Teaching pieces
0.6	Instructive editions
0.7	Two instruments
0.8	Self-instructors

Here are two examples of how the table can be applied:

Conga, Bongo, and Timbale Techniques, by David Charles
MT663.3 .C52 1982 (principally studies and exercises, with extension 0.3 from table)

Mel Bay's Deluxe Concertina Book, by Frank J. Converse
MT681.8 .C65 1981 (a self-instruction manual, with extension 0.8 from table)

Table M6: Table of Special Texts (see p. 79ff.)

Table M7: Table of Subdivisions for Regions (Cutter No.)

Table M7, a table of period subdivisions, is identical in its design to Table M3—the only difference is in its application. Whereas Table M3 has decimal extensions, M7 also accommodates for geographic subdivision through the use of a cutter. It is only used in a very few instances (for general works on South America and the Baltic States in the ML subclass).

Table M8: Table of Subdivisions for Countries (Cutter No.)

Just as Table M7 is closely related to M3, so Table M8 is like M4, in the same way. That is, Table M8 provides for a cutter/decimal extension.

Ex.:

Cuando salí de la Habana: 1898–1997: cien años de musica cubana por el mundo, by Cristóbal Díaz Ayala
ML207.C85 D53 1998 (a history of twentieth-century Cuban music; .C8 from schedule (for Cuba), with extension 5 from table, for period 1901–2000)

Katináj: estudios de etno-organología musical chaquense, by Rubén Pérez Bugallo
ML486.A77 C53 1997 (a book on musical instruments from Chaco province in Argentina; .A7 from schedule (for Argentina), with extension 7 from table (by state, province, etc., A–Z), C53 the cutter for Chaco)

Table M9: Table of Subdivisions for Countries for Popular Music (1 No.) and Table M10: Table of Subdivisions for Countries for Popular Music (Cutter No.)

These two tables are also identical except for the cutter extension in Table M10. They both apply to various spans within subclass ML, specifically, history and criticism of popular music, and both also refer to Table M1 for cuttering by U.S. regions and states as applicable. They read as follows:

Table M9 (where 0 stands for the class number in the schedule)

0.1	Addresses, essays, lectures
0.7A–Z	By state, province, etc., A–Z
	For regions and states of the United States, see Table M1
0.8A–Z	By city, A–Z

Ex.:
Island Sounds in the Global City: Caribbean Popular Music and Identity in New York, ed. by Ray Allen and Lois Wilcken
ML3477.1 .I85 1998 (extension .1 for addresses, essays, lectures)

West Coast Jazz: Modern Jazz in California, 1945–1960, by Ted Gioia
ML3508.7.C28 G5 1992 (extension .7.C28 for California)

Las tandas de Monterrey: visión retrospectíva de la farándula, by Luis Cruz Hernández
ML3485.8.M66 C78 1994 (a book on popular music in Monterrey, Mexico, with the extension .8.M66 for the city of Monterrey)

Table M10

.x	Addresses, essays, lectures
.x7A–Z	By state, province, etc.
	For regions and states of the United States, see Table M1
.x8A–Z	By city, A–Z

Ex.:

Crónicas del rock fabricado acá, by Félix Allueva
ML3487.V41 A45 1998 (.V4 from schedule, for Venezuela, with extension .x1 for addresses, essays, lectures)

Tributos aos conjuntos vocais do Rio Grande do Norte: de 1936 a 1998, by Manuel Procopio de Moura, Jr.
ML3487.B77 R56 1998 (.B7 from schedule, for Brazil, with extension 7 R56 for province of Rio Grande do Norte)

La trova rosarina, by Sergio Arboleya
ML3487.A78 R63 1998 (.A7 from schedule, for Argentina; with extension 8
R63 for city of Rosario (Santa Fe))

Index

Indexing of the schedules within LCC is generally thorough and detailed (though less so than DDC's Relative Index), and catalogers should not hesitate to consult the index for help in finding a particular class. Although LCC:M's index is quite helpful, it does not list names of performers or composers found in the schedule (e.g., Franz Liszt or Richard Wagner). One of the major advantages of the online, hypertext version, Classification Plus, is its accommodation for keyword searching. This feature, combined with the abundance of hot links within Classification Plus, makes it an extremely useful and powerful addition to the cataloger's list of resources.

NOTES

1. Leo E. LaMontagne, *American Library Classification* (Hamden, Conn.: Shoe String Press, 1961), 218; quoted in Chan, *A Guide to the Library of Congress Classification* 5th ed. (Englewood, Colo.: Libraries Unlimited, 1999), 6-7.

2. Ibid, 7.

3. Chan, *Guide to the Library of Congress Classification*, 35.

4. Ibid., 35-36.

5. Richard P. Smiraglia, *Music Cataloging* (Englewood, Colo.: Libraries Unlimited, 1989), 99.

6. In his preface to the second edition of the Class-M schedule (1917), Sonneck commented on the fact that because of these copyright deposits, as well as the Music Division's policy of "organic development," problems of classification in LC were perhaps "more numerous and more varied," than in other libraries, "at least in America."

7. *Classification, Class M, Music and Books on Music*, 2nd ed. (Washington, D.C.: Library of Congress, 1917), (3).

8. *Classification Plus*, issue 2 (Washington, D.C.: Library of Congress, Cataloging Distribution Service, 2001); and *Cataloger's Desktop*, issue 2 (Washington, D.C.: Library of Congress, Cataloging Distribution Service, 2001).

9. D. Kern Holoman, *Catalogue of the Works of Hector Berlioz* (New York: Bärenreiter, 1987).

10. For a more thorough critique of LCC:M, see Rita Benton, "The Nature of Music and some Implications for the University Music Library," *Fontes artis Musicae* 23 (1976): 53-60.

11. The Library of Congress published in 1992 its *Subject Cataloging Manual: Classification*, a formerly internal document originally intended to assist LC's own catalogers. Music is only minimally treated in this volume, however.

12. Smiraglia, xi.

13. In this sense, LCC and LCSH are complementary because LC subject headings for music give precedence to form over medium of performance.

14. Use of the term *form* is itself problematic; Chan states that "subclass M is a scheme based on physical form rather than on subject classification" (*A Guide to the Library of Congress Classification*, 322). What she actually means is an organization by *form, genre, or medium of peformance*, rather than by topic or subject.

15. And in fact, browsing the fifty-four works with the classification number M486 in the Library of Congress catalog reveals that more than half, thirty-five, are what could be considered to be early music.

16. Here is yet *another* possible classification number for early music, and an additional opportunity for discollocation!

17. On the other hand, I have found this section to be quite useful in my own library for music students who are not pianists and who need to find simple solos to play for juries or piano exams.

18. This is one case in which LCC does not seem to follow the principle for literary warrant because few, if any, separately composed cadenzas exist for instruments other than piano or violin.

19. Obviously, this note refers to music received at the Library of Congress (as copyright deposit), not in any other library!

20. Notice here that LCC:M, unlike LCSH, does *not* distinguish between musical theater works (e.g., Broadway shows), operettas, and Western European operas, so that works by Rodgers and Rossini, Gershwin and Gilbert and Sullivan, or Cole Porter and Puccini are found together in the same class.

21. The older and more commonly used term, *piano-vocal score*, is now replaced in AACR2 usage by the term *vocal score*.

22. A chorus score includes only the parts for the chorus, usually without accompaniment, and omitting the parts for soloist(s).

23. Hymnals and liturgical music that is "officially prescribed" for use in various worship traditions are discussed in a separate section on p. 89.

24. E.g., use ".G" for German, rather than ".D" for Deutsche.

25. Unaccompanied choruses are classed at M2099 with the same instructions as for M2079.

26. Notice that unlike LCSH, LCC:M makes no distinctions among songs for high, medium, or low voice.

27. The use of the term *published,* rather than *composed* here is subtle yet important because it removes the burden from the cataloger of trying to determine the actual date a song was written, and he or she can instead simply use the copyright or publisher's date on the item in hand.

28. Songs for more than one voice, often performed with one person to a part, and composed in a homophonic or chordal style with the melody in the top voice.

29. Charles Hamm, *Yesterdays: Popular Song in America* (New York: W.W. Norton, 1979): [xvii].

30. G4 cutter from Table M1 from state cutters.

31. LC does not shelflist this class.

32. Michael Gorman and Paul W. Winkler, eds., *Anglo-American Cataloguing Rules,* 2d ed., 1988 revision (Chicago: American Library Association, 1988), 376n.

33. Smiraglia, 100.

34. *Subject Cataloging Manual: Shelflisting,* 2d ed. (Washington, D.C.: Library of Congress Distribution Service, 1995); accessed via *Cataloger's Desktop* (issue 2, February 2001).

35. *Library of Congress Classification: M: Music and Books on Music,* 3d ed. (Washington, D.C.: Library of Congress, Subject Cataloging Division, 1978): 98n.

36. Smiraglia, 100.

37. Following the same order as the instruments in the other two subclasses.

38. *Library of Congress Classification: M: Music and Books on Music,* 1998 ed. (Washington, D.C.: Library of Congress, Cataloging Distribution Service, 1999), viii.

39. Ludwig van Beethoven, *32 Sonatas for the Pianoforte,* ed. Artur Schnabel (New York: Simon & Schuster), 1935.

40. Notice that this last example is first cuttered by country (.U4 for United States); while "Blue Ridge" is not listed specifically in the table, the instruction at the beginning of the table instructs us to cutter for "regions as needed in individual classes."

41. The corresponding LCSH subdivision is no longer valid.

CHAPTER 4

Alpha-Numeric System for Classification of Sound Recordings (ANSCR)

HISTORY AND BACKGROUND

Although sound recordings have long been an integral part of most music collections, they continue to present major challenges for librarians in a variety of areas, including storage, circulation, preservation, and access. Even today, libraries are oriented most heavily toward books and other printed sources. Although cataloging rules have been adapted and adjusted over the years to accommodate an ever-expanding variety of physical formats, cataloging recordings can still be problematic.

One of the greatest difficulties for librarians who catalog recordings lies in classifying them. This is primarily because so many recordings are actually collections of different works. In some cases, this fact poses no problem—a compact-disc recording of piano music, even by different composers, is classified the same as the corresponding score containing the same works. Many recordings, however, are comprised of several different genres or types of music, often by different composers and performers. A CD might include a symphonic poem by Strauss, an overture by Rossini, and a Haydn symphony; another might contain a variety of vocal, instrumental, and chamber works by several composers performed by a number of different individuals. Before the adoption of *AACR2*, these types of items were often cataloged according to the individual works they contained, so each piece on a recording might be cataloged on a separate bibliographic record. This process worked well enough for bibliographic description and access, but less well for classification. Because one function of classification is for shelf arrangement, we obviously cannot assign more than one call number to a physical item. This is one reason why so many libraries have elected not to classify their recordings at all, but have chosen some other type of organization, such as shelving by accession number or record label and label number.

These systems work adequately for closed-stack collections, but they are not as useful for libraries that permit their patrons to browse recordings on open shelves. The browsing principle remains an important function of modern libraries. LCC and DDC are not always practical for this purpose, especially with sound recordings, because of the lengthy and complex class numbers that often result in both systems. Consequently, many libraries have developed their own home-grown classification systems for recordings.

During the 1960s, a method specifically for classifying sound recordings was devised by Caroline Saheb-Ettaba and Roger B. McFarland. It was conceived chiefly as a means to facilitate browsing, especially in smaller and public libraries, where recordings are often shelved on open stacks or stored in open bins, much the way record stores arrange items for customers. This scheme was named the *Alpha-Numeric System for Classification of Sound Recordings* (ANSCR, pronounced "answer").

Saheb-Ettaba and McFarland presented the underlying principles of this system in their book, *ANSCR*, which appeared in 1969; a supplement by Linda L. Hansen was published in 1988. This work remains the principal tool for libraries that use the system. Here we will outline the principles and some of the basic applications of ANSCR, but librarians whose libraries use ANSCR should continue to consult Saheb-Ettaba and McFarland's book and the supplement for a more thorough discussion and explanation of the details of using it.

ANSCR is unlike either DDC, which is based on the universe of knowledge, or LCC, which was devised to organize the holdings of a particular library. Fundamentally a pragmatic approach, it is the only system of the three that was conceived and designed for one single medium. As the book's title page advertises, ANSCR "deals with classification of sound recordings of all types, whether on plastic disc or on tape (reel to reel, cartridge, cassette) or in any other physical format."[1] Although the scheme was devised before the advent of compact-disc recordings, ANSCR is applicable to CDs, as well as other sound-recording formats. Another important point to emphasize is that ANSCR is designed to accommodate all recordings, regardless of their content. It can be used to classify spoken-word as well as music recordings, although only the music portions of the scheme are focused on here.

OUTLINE OF THE SYSTEM

ANSCR is straightforward and logical in its overall conception and design. In their book, Saheb-Ettaba and McFarland outline the three underlying concepts that form the basis of their system: a list of broad categories ("subjects"), the "Basic Rule" that is applied in determining how an item should be classified, and the application of a unique number for each recording. As the writers state, it is in this last point that ANSCR differs from other existing classification systems, which are principally arrangements of "subject categories."[2]

An ANSCR call number consists of four elements, or "terms," each of which is notated on a separate line. These elements include the following:

Term 1: General category or subject
Term 2: Filing element for author or subcategory
Term 3: Filing element for title
Term 4: Filing element for individual recording

Although the creators identified the notation devised for the system as alphanumeric, a typical ANSCR call number is primarily alphabetical; numerals are only used in the third and fourth terms. An explanation on the construction of call numbers within ANSCR follows.

Following a description and general overview of their system, Saheb-Ettaba and McFarland present rules on the application and use of each of these terms in chapters 1–4 of their book. In this regard, ANSCR differs from the other systems covered here because LCC:M and DDC are primarily lists of class numbers, with less attention devoted to how they are to be applied (this is particularly the case with LCC:M, although DDC does include a separate manual). The classification schedule in ANSCR, on the other hand, is only one page in length, plus a few auxiliary tables for special elements. The remainder of the book is comprised primarily of rules for the application of the system's main concepts, with many examples.

Term 1: General Category or Subject

The original scheme upon which ANSCR is based consisted of thirty-six subject categories that primarily reflect medium of performance, or general style or type of music. The 1988 supplement includes an up-dated list of some expanded categories (indicated in the following list by an asterisk), but the general design of the scheme remains the same. These subjects are notated in Term 1 and are represented by one or two letters. Notice in Fig. 4-1 that there are a limited number of hierarchies, only one or two levels, throughout the entire scheme (main categories that have subcategories are never used alone).

A	Music Appreciation— History and Commentary	MG	Contemporary Christian/Gospel*
B	Operas: Complete and Highlights	MJ	Jazz
		MR	Rock, Rhythm
C	Choral Music		and Blues, etc.*
D	Vocal Music	P	Folk and Ethnic Music—
E	Orchestral Music		National
EA	General Orchestral	Q	International Folk
EB	Ballet Music		and Ethnic Music
EC	Concertos	R	Holiday Music
ES	Symphonies	S	Varieties and Humor: (Comic
F	Chamber Music		Monologs, Musical Satire,
G	Solo Instrumental Music		Comedy Acts, Etc.)
GG	Guitar	SR	Radio Transcriptions
		ST	Television Transcriptions*
GO	Organ	T	Plays
GP	Piano	U	Poetry
GS	Stringed Instruments	V	Prose
GV	Violin	W	Documentary: History
GW	Wind Instruments		and Commentary
GX	Percussion Instruments	X	Instructional: (Dictation
H	Band Music		Languages, "How to . . .,"
J	Electronic, Mechanical Music		Etc.)
K	Musical Shows and Operettas: Complete and Excerpts	Y	Sounds and Special Effects
		Z	Children's Recordings:
L	Soundtrack Music: Motion Pictures and Television	ZI	Instructional
		ZM	Music
M	Popular Music	ZR	Holiday Music*
MA	Pop Music	ZS	Spoken
MC	Country and Western Music		

Figure 4-1 List of ANSCR Class Numbers

A brief perusal of this classification schedule reveals its overall plan: all vocal music comes together, followed by instrumental music of various types; then assorted categories of popular formats (with musicals and operettas, as a result, separated from other vocal music); spoken-word recordings; and finally, children's recordings, the list of which was also modified in the 1988 supplement, and now includes more than one additional subcategory of children's music. These are all broad, very simple (some might even say simplistic) categories, especially when compared with the complex and detailed varieties of types of music that LCC:M and DDC 780 are capable of classifying. Although the authors claim that the ANSCR symbols in Term 1 are not mnemonic, there is, in fact, some alphabetic correspondence in the subclasses (EB for ballets, GS for stringed instruments, MJ for jazz, etc.).

Although these various categories might seem fairly logical, upon closer scrutiny we can identify a variety of situations in which they might not function as adequately for the libraries they are meant to serve as other systems might. One major area is class M, popular music, no doubt one of the most heavily collected and widely circulating categories of recordings in most public libraries today. The original version of ANSCR allowed for only three subcategories, pop (MA), country and western (MC), and jazz (MJ), which many library users no doubt found less than adequate in browsing for their particular favorite styles of music. The authors defended their decision to limit the number of subcategories on the grounds that trends in popular music are volatile and constantly changing. They asserted that the "lines of distinction between blues, rhythm and blues, rock, folk rock, pop rock, jazz rock, hard rock, soft rock, swing, be bop, cool jazz, Dixie jazz [sic], to mention only a few, are largely a matter of personal taste and interpretation."[3] Most fans of these various styles of music would probably disagree. On the other hand, it might be argued that the majority of users usually know what they want and less frequently search by subject or browse in categories. As long as ANSCR keeps all of the Miles Davis, Dolly Parton, Aerosmith, or Pat Boone recordings together in their respective sequences, perhaps most patrons will be satisfied.

It should also be emphasized that the changes to the scheme that were made in the 1988 supplement have improved it greatly, especially for popular music, and most libraries have adopted these changes. Also, libraries may always (and frequently do) modify any existing scheme for their own particular needs. A search on the World Wide Web for libraries that use ANSCR showed that the system has been adapted in a number of different ways for local use, although most libraries that use ANSCR seem to maintain its general structure.

Popular music is not the only category in ANSCR that requires some explanation, or that differs from LCC or DDC. Class D, vocal music, is set aside for music for solo voice, with or without accompaniment, as well as for vocal chamber works (duets, trios, quartets, etc.) that involve one singer per part. The exceptions are opera excerpts, such as collections of arias, which are classed in B, operas and opera highlights, and operetta and musical comedy arias and songs, which are classed in K. Popular vocal recordings are found within M, with other popular music. Recordings of Gregorian and other types of chant of the early Christian church are classed with A, music appreciation—history and commentary, rather than with choral music, category C.

Unlike LCC:M and LCSH, which apply the term *solo instrumental music* literally (music for only one instrument, without accompaniment), ANSCR includes in category G music for solo instrument "with or without accompaniment of another instrument." This is actually how most people think of solo literature, so, in this instance, ANSCR is probably more in keeping with the way the public would search for these materials. ANSCR defines chamber music as any work "written for, or performed by, instrumental groups of not less than three nor more than nine instruments, and in which only one player is assigned to each part."[4] The category includes all instrumental media, without any further subdivision, so that patrons looking for string quartets, for example, will have to browse through the entire category to find them all. Chamber orchestras, string ensembles of larger than nine instruments, and other similar groups, are all classed with full orchestras within E, orchestral music; and wind ensembles that are comprised of more than nine instruments are found in H, band music.

Categories P and Q comprise what we would refer to today as *world music*; the terms "folk" and "ethnic" have, to a large extent, become outmoded and are considered by many to be exclusionary. The categories themselves remain valid, nonetheless, because there remains a strong demand for these various types of traditional music. *National* in this sense refers to American folk music, regardless of its place of origin (notice that LCC:M applies the term *national music* in a more generic sense to mean music of any given country). ANSCR also classes in category P "contemporary 'folk' music" (the kind that was so prevalent in the '60s, when the scheme was being formed—including recordings by such performers as Bob Dylan, Judy Collins, Joan Baez, etc.), rather than in category M. This illustrates one of the greatest difficulties in classifying these various types of vernacular music—many times musical styles and categories blur ("crossover" is another term for it) and ANSCR equivocates in several instances in its instructions on where to class various types of music.

Basic Rule

Before a category can be selected for a recording, the cataloger must evaluate the recording according to ANSCR's "Basic Rule" of classification, which reads as follows:

Discs
If the first work on side one of the disc occupies one-third or more of the space on side one, the recording is classed according to the type or form of this first work. If the first work on side one does not occupy one-third or more of the space on side one, the entire recording is examined for general content in order to determine its classification.

Tapes
If the first work on side one of the tape occupies one-third or more of the time on side one, the recording is classed according to the type or form of this first work. If the first work on side one does not occupy one-third or more of the time on side one, the entire recording is examined for general content in order to determine its classification.[5]

In other words, the classifying element in Term 1 is determined from the first work on the item. If this appears to be a prominent work (one-third of the duration of the side), the recording is classified according to this work. If not, the recording is treated collectively based on the nature of the entire recording. An exception to the basic rule occurs when a "featured work" appears elsewhere than on side one, band one. In this situation, the rules allow the recording to be classified according to a work that is other than the first work on side one, if the typography, layout, or design of the album signify that this work is a "featured" work, and provided that it occupies one-third of a side of a recording. Although the "exception" rule does not address tapes, we can assume that it applies in these situations as well. What about CDs? Compact discs are obviously the recording medium of choice among today's library patrons. Many libraries have even discarded their LP and tape collections, or else relegated them to remote storage. The advent of new formats (not to mention new styles and genres of music) illustrates one of the shortcomings of classification schemes, such as ANSCR, that are more utilitarian than systematic in their conception. Such methods often are not as capable of accommodating change. We can probably infer, however, that CDs would be subject to the same principle as that for tapes, which are also classed according to duration, rather than the width of the first band as on an LP. The main difference in CDs is that only one side is "played," so we must modify the rule accordingly.

Term 2: Filing Element for Author or Subcategory

Term 2 of an ANSCR call number consists of four letters derived from a surname, title, name of country, or other identifying characteristic of a recording. We might consider this term, or filing element, to be analogous to the cutter number or author number of an LC or Dewey call number. The principle behind all of these methods is that of collocation, one of the main ways libraries accommodate browsing. We want all of the recordings of Brahms symphonies, Bach cantatas, or performances by Ella Fitzgerald together in an intuitive or logical sequence.

In ANSCR, Term 2 is somewhat more flexible than the corresponding cutter number in LCC or DDC. The choice of this filing element is based, in part, on the overall nature of the recording; depending on the main category chosen, the term can be derived from the composer, principal performer, or title. ANSCR identifies thirteen different ways of organizing recordings within term 2. The term is selected according to the content or nature of the recording. These thirteen entry choices are as follows:

Composer entry	Gregorian entry
Author entry	Instructional subject entry
Performer entry	Language entry
Title entry	Person-as-subject entry

Bible entry   Sounds entry (i.e., special effects)
Ethnic entry

An additional term is used for miscellaneous collections when none of the above entries is applicable.

Composer Entry

The first four of the entries are those most commonly used, especially for musical recordings; some of the others are more applicable to non-music recordings. The first type of entry, composer entry, is used for most recordings of Western art music, when the corresponding main entry is by composer, and following the application of the Basic Rule (the "one-third" rule). Here are some representative examples:

Piano Concertos K. 246 in C major and K. 414 in A major by W. A. Mozart:
Term 1: EC
Term 2: MOZA

Fanfare for the Common Man and *A Lincoln Portrait*, by Aaron Copland (side 1)
Three Places in New England, by Charles Ives (side 2)
Term 1: EA
Term 2: COPL
(Here apply "the one-half" rule of Term 2 (204-B2), which states that if the first half of the whole recording (for LPs or cassettes) is devoted to one or more than one work by one composer, use that composer's surname to form Term 2.)

Because of the complexity of some composers' names, ANSCR also offers a useful table that lists names of many composers with the corresponding four-to-six-letter abbreviations, as well as a detailed set of instructions on how to formulate the Term 2 element for composers' names not on the list. In some cases, an additional distinguishing letter must be added for similar or identical surnames. With musical families, the less-famous members of the family are assigned extensions, as in the following examples:

Bach, Johann Sebastian   **BACH**
Bach, Carl Philipp Emanuel   **BACH-C**

| Schumann, Robert | SCHUM |
| Schumann, Clara | SCHUM-C |

Performer Entry

Entry by performer in Term 2 is reserved primarily for popular recordings, in particular, those in category M, as well as recordings of the Boston Pops and of concert and marching bands, if the rules for composer entry do not apply. The entry element for performer is formed in the same manner as for composer entries. ANSCR does not include a list of performers' names with abbreviations, however, as it does with composers. This is because of the "ephemeral" nature of most popular music collections within libraries. According to ANSCR rule 206-C7, there is no need to differentiate between performers, except within categories. The rule also suggests the establishment and maintenance of an authority file so that, as performers' names are withdrawn, the abbreviation for their names can be reassigned to new performers. The following are representative examples of performer entries:

Butterfly, by Barbra Streisand
Term 1: MA
Term 2: STRE

Cool Water, by the Sons of the Pioneers
Term 1: MC
Term 2: SONS

Gems of the Concert Band, by the Detroit Concert Band
Term 1: H
Term 2: DETR

Title Entry

According to ANSCR rule 207-B, entry by title for Term 2 applies when "the album title is the quickest and most satisfactory tool in retrieving the desired recording."[6] Because it was thought that most people would not know composers of musical shows or of motion picture soundtracks, ANSCR prescribes title entry for these categories (K and

L), as well as for documentaries (W). It might be argued that many people *would* search under "Rodgers, Richard" for recordings of the musical *Oklahoma*, for example, because the show is usually cataloged with the composer's name as the main entry. Title entry in Term 2 is also used in class A, music appreciation anthologies, etc., which by definition are all collections.

Title entry elements are formed in much the same manner as other types of entries, by taking the first four letters of the title (using as many words, excluding articles and prepositions after the first word, as is necessary). In recordings where the Term 2 element is identical, we are instructed to make no differentiation among the entries. Examples of title entry in Term 2 include the following:

Les misérables, by Alain Boublil and Claude-Michel Schönberg (musical show)
Term 1: K
Term 2: MISE

Braveheart: original motion picture soundtrack, music composed and conducted by James Horner
Term 1: L
Term 2: BRAV

Songs of the Troubadours & Trouvères: Music and poetry from Medieval France.
Term 1: A
Term 2: SONG

Breakfast at Tiffany's: original motion picture soundtrack, by Henry Mancini
Term 1: L
Term 2: BREA

The Breakfast Club: original motion picture soundtrack
Term 1: L
Term 2: BREA

On the Town, by Leonard Bernstein, Betty Comden, and Adolph Green
Term 1: K
Term 2: ONTO

On the Twentieth Century, by Cy Coleman, Betty Comden, and Adolph Green
Term 1: K
Term 2: ONTW

Collections Entry

Although we might consider the majority of recordings to be collections because, by and large, they contain more than one work, ANSCR defines a collection somewhat more narrowly. According to rule 208-B1, a collection is a recording containing "a number of works by different composers or authors, and in which the purpose of the recording is to feature the type of material selected, rather than the special talents of individuals, such as composers, performers, etc."[7] Most of the recordings that fall under this definition, then, are those that contain a number of different works by more than one composer performed by more than one performer.[8] The rule states further that entry under collection may be used only in cases in which entry under composer, performer, or title does not apply.

The entry element in Term 2 for these types of recordings is the four-letter abbreviation COLL. This entry could, in some cases, conflict with other names or titles that begin with the same letters. In these cases, an additional distinguishing letter must be added to those entries. Following are some examples of these applications:

Smithsonian Collection of Classic Jazz
Term 1: MJ
Term 2: COLL

Angels' Visits: and other Vocal Gems of Victorian America
Term 1: D
Term 2: COLL

Blues Classics 1927-1969
Term 1: MJ
Term 2: COLL

Live '92-'93, by Albert Collins and the Icebreakers.
Term 1: MJ
Term 2: COLL-A

Ethnic and Geographic Entries

ANSCR prescribes eight other types of entries in Term 2 that it calls "subject entries," in addition to the five listed above. Ethnic entry is prescribed for use in Term 2 of category P (only) for four ethnic groups in the U.S. These groups with their abbreviations include the following:

Ethnic Group	Entry Element
Cajun	CAJUN
Hawaiian	HAWA
Indian (i.e., native American)	INDI
Eskimo	ESKI

Recordings classed in category P that do not fall under the rules for performer or ethnic entry should be entered as collections:

J'ai été au bal = I Went to the Dance: the Cajun and Zydeco Music of Louisiana
Term 1: P
Term 2: CAJUN

Songs of Earth, Water, Fire, and Sky: Music of the American Indian
Term 1: P
Term 2: INDI

Voices from the American South
Term 1: P
Term 2: COLL

Recordings of folk and traditional music of other countries are classed in category Q. ANSCR assigns popular music of other countries to category M, but acknowledges that it is sometimes difficult to discern whether some recordings are more popular or traditional in nature. This is perhaps even more a concern today than when the scheme was developed, since many regions around the world now have very active commercial-music industries. ANSCR states that in cases of doubt, class Q should be chosen, since most persons interested in recordings from these countries are more interested in the national or ethnic facet than the style or genre of the music.

The Term 2 element for recordings classed in Q is based on country or geographic area, depending on the focus of the recording. ANSCR prescribes geographic entry for use only with category Q. The entry element is derived from a table (Q-3C) that lists abbreviations for more than 160 countries (including colonies and territorial dependencies); this includes a number of cross-references (e.g., England, Scotland, Ireland, Northern Ireland, and Wales are listed under British Isles). The rule (Q-3A) states that countries in the table are given as they exist "at the present time." This list is obviously outdated (U.S.S.R. and East and West Germany are two prime examples). Besides entry by country, ANSCR allows for classification by broader geographic areas in a few instances:

Area	Entry Term
Africa	AFRICA
Asia	ASIA
Europe	EUROPE
Latin America	LATIN
Near and Middle East	EAST

In addition, three styles of music that ANSCR identifies as "transcending national boundaries [or having] no fixed general geographic area" may be used as entry elements:

Style	Entry Term
Calypso	CALY
Gypsy	GYPS
Yiddish	YIDD

If none of the rules for entry by geographic term apply within category Q, ANSCR instructs us to use the COLL entry element instead. The following examples show how the geographic entry is used with category Q:

Music in the Mind: the Concept of Music and Musician in Afghanistan
Term 1: Q
Term 2: AFGH

Popular and Folk Songs of Latin America, performed by Los Indios Tabajaras
Term 1: Q
Term 2: LATI

The Alan Lomax Collection Sampler
Term 1: Q
Term 2: COLL

Gregorian Entry

ANSCR includes Gregorian and similar types of chants with music appreciation and historical anthologies of music in class A. Because this category consists of collections by definition, using the entry element COLL in Term 2 would be redundant for call numbers in this category. The scheme, therefore, collocates all chant recordings in a single file with the Term 2 entry element GREG. For example:

Gregorian Chant Liturgy for Good Friday, performed by the Gregorian Choir of Paris
Term 1: A
Term 2: GREG

Sarum Chant: Salisbury Psalmodie
Term 1: A
Term 2: GREG

Series Entry

In those instances where a recording comprises part of a series, AN-SCR prescribes a series entry element in Term 2. The individual album title is then entered in Term 3.

Term 3: Filing Element for Title

After a recording has been placed in a general subject or category (Term 1) and marked according to composer or other distinctive characteristic (Term 2), the next step in deriving a unique ANSCR call number is to assign a filing element for title (Term 3). Here ANSCR's terminology can get rather confusing because, as we have seen, a title might also be used as a filing element in Term 2 for some categories of recordings. In defining Term 3 as the title element, ANSCR demonstrates its orientation toward recordings of Western art music and a certain inflexibility with respect to other categories of recordings.

The issue of title is complex with recordings, more so than with books. Books, by and large, have only one title, and that title is clearly stated on the title page. A recording, on the other hand, might have a collective title for the entire item (ANSCR refers to this to as the "album" title), in addition to individual titles for each of the works it contains. In light of these distinctions, ANSCR identifies two types of titles, album (or collective) titles, and work titles, which are the titles of the individual compositions contained on a recording. In some cases, these might be identical (for example, if a recording includes only one large-scale work, such as an opera or musical).

Work titles themselves may fall into one of two categories: distinctive titles (e.g., *La mer, Peter and the Wolf,* or *Ave Maria*), or generic or nondistinctive titles that identify the type or form of composition (e.g., Brahms's Violin Concerto in D major, op. 35, or the Mass in C, K. 317, by Mozart). ANSCR does not allow nicknames or popular titles for generic works to be used in forming the title element in term 3 (even though many people might prefer to search for Beethoven's "Moonlight" Sonata or Schubert's "Trout" Quintet, rather than the official generic title).

Several ways of deriving the title element for a recording are covered in Term 3. For collective or album titles, the title element in Term 3 is formed by taking the initial letters of the significant words in the title, up to three, and excluding articles and prepositions. For titles consisting only of one significant word, we are instructed to use the first three consecutive letters of the title. Performers' names in full appearing at the beginning of album titles are to be disregarded. Term 3 might sometimes seem superfluous, as in the case of categories K (musical shows) and L (movie soundtracks), which are already entered by their titles in Term 2. Because titles are abbreviated differently in these two terms, the appearance of redundancy is lessened, but because every ANSCR call number *must* contain four terms, the duplication still exists, and Term 3 might really be unnecessary.

Deriving a work title element for Term 3 depends on the nature of the work. Distinctive titles are abbreviated in the same manner as album titles. If the title is in a foreign language, particularly German or a Romance language, the same rules apply as for titles in English, that is, all articles and prepositions after the first word are omitted. If a title is in any other language or is transliterated, articles and prepositions are included in the abbreviation. If a work with a distinctive title in a foreign language is more commonly known by its English title, we are instructed *always* to use the English form of the title, regardless of the title on the item, and even if it conflicts with the uniform title in the cataloging record.

Nondistinctive or generic title elements are taken from the first three letters of the compositional form or genre, followed by some type of number. ANSCR rule 306-B2 includes a table of two- or three-letter abbreviations for the most common music forms and genres. ANSCR identifies four types of numbers that are found in musical works. These are given as follows in order of preference for their use in deriving the entry element for Term 3 (and excluding the sub-opus number, which is never used):

1. Opus numbers—Numbers assigned in a consecutive sequence by the composer or original publisher.
2. Sub-opus numbers—Numbers assigned for individual works that are published as parts of sets under a single opus number.
3. Form numbers—Serial numbers that identify chronological order of composition within a particular genre, such as Symphony no. 8 or String Quartet no. 17.
4. Thematic catalog numbers—Numbers assigned by a scholar or other compiler of a composer's complete works. These types of numbers are especially useful for certain prolific composers whose works may lack opus numbers. ANSCR also refers to this as the musicologist's number.[9]

The types of numbers are, in most cases, used in combination with the form abbreviations in table 306-B2, but if the entry element in Term 1 consists of a type of work (EC, concerto, or ES, symphony), then the number by itself is all that is needed. Here are some examples of title entries in Term 3:

Album title entry
Welcome to Vienna (Beverly Sills, soprano)
Term 1: C
Term 2: SILL
Term 3: WV

Album title entry with series
Series: *Alan Lomax Collection*
Album title: *Ozark Frontier*
Term 1: P
Term 2: ALAN
Term 3: OF

Work title entry: Musical show
Album title: *Rodgers & Hammerstein's The Sound of Music*
Work title: Sound of Music
Term 1: K
Term 2: SOUN
Term 3: SM

Work title entry: distinctive title in English
Album title: *Death in Venice* / Benjamin Britten
Uniform title: Death in Venice
Term 1: B
Term 2: BRIT
Term 3: DV

Work title entry: distinctive title in French
Album, work, and uniform titles: *Poème de l'amour et de la mer* / Ernest Chausson
Term 1: C
Term 2: CHAU
Term 3: PAE

Work title entry: generic title with number-only entry element in Term 3
Album title: *Piano Concerto no. 1* / music by Frédéric Chopin
Uniform title: Concertos, piano, orchestra, no. 1, op. 11, E minor
Term 1: EC
Term 2: CHOP
Term 3: 1

Work title entry: generic title with title-thematic catalog entry element in Term 3
Album title: *Serenade in D, K. 250: Haffner-Serenade* / W.A. Mozart
Uniform title: Serenades, K. 250, D major
Term 1: EA
Term 2: MOZA
Term 3: SER-250

Work title entry: generic title entry with additional distinctive title
Album title: *Cantata no. 140: Wachet auf, ruft uns die Stimme* / J. S. Bach
Uniform title: Wachet auf, ruft uns die Stimme
Term 1: C
Term 2: BACH
Term 3: CAN-140[10]

Work title entry: work with both generic title and popular title
Album title: *Quartet no. 14 in D minor: Death and the Maiden* / Franz Schubert
Uniform title: Quartets, strings, D. 810, D minor
Term 1: F
Term 2: SCHUB
Term 3: QS-14

Work title entry in Russian; entry under common English title
Album title: *George Balanchine's The Nutcracker* / music by Peter Ilich Tchaikovsky
Uniform title: Shchelkunchik
Term 1: EB
Term 2: TCHA
Term 3: NUT

Term 4: Filing Element for Individual Recording

As with the other classification systems, one of the primary functions of ANSCR is to provide a scheme for classifying recordings based on their content, which ANSCR accomplishes through the first three terms of its call number structure. An additional goal of ANSCR is to offer a means of differentiating among similar recordings by creating a distinctive call number for each individual recording. This is the purpose of Term 4, which includes information that identifies a particular recording through the employment of three alphanumeric characters derived from the individual item. In many instances, this information might not be necessary because the first three terms are enough to identify a particular recording. On the other hand, a library might own several different recordings of the same work, performed by different performers and issued on different record labels.

Although the Library of Congress often uses a date at the end of an LCC call number to distinguish among similar works, this is not always possible with recordings, especially LPs, which less frequently bear dates of publication or issue. Instead, ANSCR has devised a system of one letter (or "alpha symbol" in ANSCR terminology) derived from the name of an individual or group associated prominently with the recording, and two numbers taken from the last two digits of the record label, or manufacturer's, number. These last two digits should exclude the final "check digit" used by many companies for distinguishing among compact disc, LP, and cassette versions of the same recording.[11] If it is not possible to use an individual's name for the entry element, the first letter of the record label may be used instead. Here are some representative examples:

Symphony no. 35 in D, K. 385: "Haffner" / W. A. Mozart. Orchestra of the 18th Century, Franz Brüggen, conductor. Philips: 416 490-2
Term 1: ES
Term 2: MOZA
Term 3: 35
Term 4: B 90

String Quartet no. 12 in F major, op. 96: the "American" Quartet / Antonín Dvořák. Chilingirian Quartet. Chandos: CHAN 8919
Term 1: F
Term 2: DVOR
Term 3: QS-12
Term 4: C 19

Masterpieces of Music before 1750. Various performers. Haydn Society: HSE 9038-9040
Term 1: A
Term 2: MAST
Term 3: MMS
Term 4: H 40

NOTES

1. Caroline Saheb-Ettaba and Roger B. McFarland, *ANSCR: the Alpha-Numeric System for Classification of Recordings* (Williamsport, Pa.: Bro-Dart Publishing Co., 1969), [iii].
2. Ibid., xvi.

3. Ibid., 13.
4. Ibid., 65.
5. Ibid., 4-5.
6. Ibid., 143.
7. Ibid., 144.
8. This category of works corresponds to the type of work that receives a title main entry under AACR2.
9. This is the same order of preference prescribed in AACR2 for constructing uniform titles.
10. ANSCR prescribes the use of the distinctive title to form Term 3 only if there is no serial or form number.
11. For recordings with no label number, some libraries use 00; if an ISBN is present, it may serve as a substitute for the manufacturer's number.

CHAPTER 5

Shelf Arrangement in the Classification
of Music Materials

INTRODUCTION

One of the main purposes of any classification process is ensuring that items are arranged for retrieval in an intuitive and logical sequence. Thus far, much emphasis has been placed on the collocating function of classification—that is, being certain that similar works are found together on the shelf. It is also important, however, that library users be able to distinguish between similar items and locate from among all of a library's holdings the item or items that most closely match their needs. Not only do we expect to find all piano sonatas in the same location, and Beethoven's piano sonatas shelved together, but we also want to be able to distinguish quickly and easily among all of the different editions of Beethoven sonatas the library owns. An effective shelf arrangement system, therefore, complements a library's catalog by providing users with the means to differentiate among all of these various facets, and to select and retrieve needed materials in an efficient and timely manner.

The principal goal of both DDC and LCC is to classify works according to their intellectual content; neither system is designed to address the issue of shelf organization for items after they have been classed. As a result, libraries have devised or adopted many ways of marking and shelving their materials. Most of these methods are based on some variation of a system conceived by Charles Cutter that was originally part of his Expansive Classification. Cutter devised a table of alphanumeric symbols that are added to classification numbers so that items within a class can be shelved in a logical sequence, in this case, alphabetically by author or title. The table is known as a *cutter table*, and the symbol, comprised of a series of letters and numbers, is known as the *cutter number* (or sometimes the book or author number). Libraries that use DDC usually employ any one of a number of versions of Cutter's original two-figure table or a similar three-figure table, later devised by Kate E. Sanborn and referred to as the *Cutter-Sanborn table* (subsequently revised by Paul K. Swanson and Esther M. Swift). The Library of Congress created its own series of tables that somewhat resemble Charles Cutter's original plan, but have been adapted for LC's own collections.

A complete call number for any given item, therefore, includes not only the DDC or LCC class number constructed from the appropriate schedule, but also a cutter number that uniquely identifies it and allows for more efficient retrieval. Because shelf arrangement, or shelflisting, is highly localized, we will only discuss the process in general terms, and refer readers to other sources that provide more detailed information regarding various shelflisting processes. As can be recalled from our discussion of ANSCR, the construction of an ANSCR call number includes formulating an entry element for the specific recording (Term 4); this procedure is much the same as shelflisting.

SHELF ARRANGEMENT IN DDC

Libraries that class their materials according to DDC most commonly use work or author numbers derived from Cutter or Cutter-Sanborn tables in creating call numbers. Cutter's shelf-arrangement system is, of course, oriented toward books rather than music, but it functions adequately enough for musical works—especially for those bearing distinctive titles. Some modifications must be made for nondistinctive or generic titles, however, as well as for sound recordings in general. Cutter numbers consist of the following three elements:

1. The initial letter of the main entry (usually a surname)
2. Two or three digits that allow placement in an alphabetical sequence
3. A lowercase letter that represents the first significant word in the title

For vowels and the letter S, use the first two letters of the name; three letters are used for names beginning with Sc. An example of the Cutter number for Verdi's *La traviata* would be .V484t (remember that the number is filed as a decimal). The digits 484 are derived from the Cutter or Cutter-Sanborn tables, which are comprised of alphabetical ranges representing the beginnings of names that correspond with numerical sequences of two or three digits. For example:

Verc	**481**
Verci	**482**
Verd	**483**
Verdi	**484**
Verdig	**485**
Verdo	**486**
Verdu	**487**
Verdy	**488**
Vere	**489**

As is evident, the three-digit number for names beginning with Verdi- (including Giuseppe Verdi!) are all cuttered .V484; the cutter number for the Renaissance composer Philippe Verdelot is .V483, etc.

Libraries have had to make modifications in call numbers for music materials in a number of ways. Many music collections include more than one edition of the score of *La traviata*, for example, as well as several different recordings of the opera. Libraries might choose, therefore, to add to the cutter number the date of the edition or recording, or letters for other names associated with the edition or recording (for publisher, record label, conductor of performance, etc.). Creating cutter numbers for works with nondistinctive or generic titles also requires modifying the system. A common practice in many libraries is to add opus or serial numbers as well as a date or cutter for publisher, editor, etc., to make the call number distinctive.

SHELF ARRANGEMENT IN LCC

As shown, LCC uses a cuttering system extensively in the Class-M schedule for a variety of situations, particularly for A–Z subarrangements within a single class number. The Library of Congress also uses this cuttering system for shelf arrangement in much the way cutter numbers are used with DDC.[1] Some differences, however, are explained in the following section. Also, the Library of Congress does not use LCC for organizing its own collections of sound recordings, but instead shelves them by label and label number. For a number of years, LC's catalogers provided class numbers in brackets in the catalog records for their recordings. As Richard Smiraglia has observed, with the advent of the AACR2 unit description and performer main entry for sound recordings in 1981, classification of collective works has become easier. Libraries should find that LCC can now be accommodated to their recording collections much more easily than in the past.[2]

Several informative and helpful works on creating call numbers with LCC have been published. Two of the most valuable are Smiraglia's *Shelflisting Music: Guidelines for Use with the Library of Congress Classification: M* and the *Subject Cataloging Manual: Shelflisting*, prepared by the Cataloging Policy and Support Office of the Library of Congress (also available in electronic form in Cataloger's Desktop). Detailed instructions on shelflisting in LCC are found in section G 800 of the latter work, which also includes an introductory paragraph that discusses the background of shelflisting at LC:

The music shelflist was begun in the Music Division in 1904. At that time, a system of Cuttering, different from that used in other classes, was devised for subclasses M, ML, and MT. As a part of the transfer of music cataloging from the Music Division to the Processing Department, the music shelflist was transferred in 1943 to the Subject Cataloging Division, where the main part of the shelflist was housed. There was an effort made to coordinate music shelflisting methods with those used in the main shelflist. The result was that new methods of shelflisting were created, adding to those inherited from the Music Division. Several methods of Cuttering may be found in the same class, and it is sometimes difficult to determine which pattern to follow when a new entry is introduced. In 1957, when the then Music Section was established, the music shelflist was moved to the Descriptive Cataloging Division. The Music Section performed the descriptive and subject cataloging, as well as the shelflisting, of most music materials. After the cataloging reorganization of 1992, this arrangement continued, with the music teams of the Special Materials Cataloging Division replacing the former Music Section. Many revisions of shelflisting processes have been made in an effort to improve, simplify, and rationalize the work. Where the introduction of new procedures would have meant extensive changes to older entries, new entries were made to fit into the old system. For example, if some of a composer's works are provided with opus numbers, some with serial numbers, and still others with keys, three methods of shelflisting may be found, not only in the same class but for the same composer. Because of the volume of music published and received by the Library of Congress, not all items cataloged receive full call numbers.

These materials fall into the category known as un-Cuttered classes. Books about music are shelflisted following the provisions for shelflisting other materials at the Library of Congress. This instruction sheet provides guidance in the shelflisting of music materials.[3]

This paragraph explains the history of shelflisting practice for music materials at LC, a practice that has not only varied within LC, but that also differs from the cutter method used with DDC. For works entered under composer or author, rather than adding a small letter at the end of the cutter number for the title, the title is cuttered separately, usually on the line below the author number. For example, the call number for Verdi's *La traviata* in LCC might look something like this:

M
1500 (class number for operas)
.V48   (cutter for Verdi)
 T52   (cutter for Traviata)

Works with generic titles usually only receive the work number for composer, with an additional distinguishing element, such as an opus or thematic catalog number, or key, rather than a cutter for title. For example:

Sonatina in G Major, Op. 100, by Antonín Dvořák
M
219
.D86
op. 100

Third Sonata in A, for Violin and Piano, by Ross Lee Finney
M
219
.F55
no.3

Sonate pour violin & piano, by Claude Debussy [in G minor]
M
219
.D29
Gmin.

In these three examples, the title of the work equates to the classification, so a title cutter would be superfluous. If there is no need for differentiation (e.g., a composer only composed one violin sonata), a single author cutter is sufficient:

> *Sonatina for Violin and Piano*, by Roque Cordero
> M
> 219
> .C7

Any other elements that are necessary to distinguish among various manifestations of the same work can also be added. One element in particular is the date; a 1982 policy change required the addition of the imprint date to all monographic (i.e., nonserial) works. LC also distinguishes among translations of works by adding digits to the title cutter number. These are derived from a special music translation table. The Library of Congress also uses its own series of work number tables, which are simpler than the two- or three-figure Cutter or Cutter-Sanborn tables used for DDC. These tables are located in the Library of Congress *Cataloging Service Bulletin* (no. 3, p. 20) or in section G 60 of the *Subject Cataloging Manual: Shelflisting*. Smiraglia's *Shelflisting Music* also reprints these tables, and provides a set of clear and concise step-by-step guidelines for formulating call numbers within LCC, together with a useful flow chart that outlines the entire process. Although this pamphlet is out of print, it remains a most useful tool for catalogers who deal with LCC.

Although the LC cuttering is simpler in many ways because it is based on the principle of literary warrant, the Cutter-Sanborn table is, in other respects, more user-friendly because it is "fixed," rather than "relative"; in other words, the cutter number for Verdi in LC varies from class to class, although it remains constant within the Cutter-Sanborn system, regardless of the classification number.

The Library of Congress has chosen not to shelflist some classes of materials with complete call numbers, other than an intial cutter letter for composer after the class number. These types of works include individual secular songs, separate works for piano, etc. Searching for Betsy Jolas's piano piece *Calling E.C.* in the Library of Congress online catalog, therefore, gives us the call number M25.J, and for Amy Beach's set of songs, *Mother Songs*, M1621.B.

NOTES

1. Remember that this system is separate from LCC; procedures for shelflisting all materials are delineated in the *Subject Cataloging Manual: Shelflisting*.

2. Smiraglia, *Music Cataloging*, 99.

3. *Subject Cataloging Manual: Shelflisting*. Library of Congress Cataloging Policy and Support Office. *Subject Cataloging Manual: Shelflisting* (Washington, D.C.: The Office, 1995), xxx.

CHAPTER 6

Concluding Observations

As Richard Smiraglia has written, classification might be the most complex yet least well-developed activity in the bibliographic control of music materials.[1] Many of these complexities have been covered in this manual. Previous chapters have illustrated how different systems have attempted to deal with the special problems music presents in a variety of ways and from a number of perspectives. The Dewey Decimal Classification system, as shown, represents a global approach to classification, reflecting as it does Melvil Dewey's ideas regarding the organization of knowledge in a systematic fashion, where music is just one component among a whole universe of disciplines. As observed, the "differentness" of music has sometimes created difficulties for classification in DDC because of the problems of format and the need to separate music compositions from the works written about them. Libraries that use DDC have nevertheless been successful in adapting the system in a variety of ways to serve the needs of music users.

DDC is produced under the aegis of the Decimal Classification Editorial Policy Committee (EPC), a ten-member international board comprised of representatives from all types of libraries, including the Library of Congress, the Library Association of Great Britain, as well as the American Library Association, OCLC Forest Press, and library educators. That DDC's editors are committed to keeping the system current and up to date is witnessed by the appearance of the DDC 20 Phoenix schedule, which greatly improved the system's organization of music. DDC 20 removed much of the pervading Western-art bias of the previous editions and created better access to non-Western and Western vernacular music genres and styles. The fact that DDC is continually being upgraded and improved presents both benefits and challenges for libraries, which often lack the resources to implement these changes. Even though such revisions are much simpler to make now with electronic databases, the physical relabeling and shifting of existing collections remain hindrances to totally effective reclassification for many libraries.

Another distinguishing feature of DDC, especially in comparison with the Library of Congress Classification system, is the faceted nature of its structure, which is emphasized to an even greater degree in the Phoenix revision. Number building (notational synthesis) represents an economical method for constructing classification numbers and ensures greater consistency within the entire system. It facilitates browsing and offers the possibility for enhanced online retrieval, particularly if the system were able somehow to be linked with a thesaurus to permit users to combine individual terms through postcoordinate indexing.

From a practical point of view, however, the faceted nature of DDC can result in some extremely lengthy numbers, even though it can provide a very detailed and accurate description of a work—especially when compared with LCC.[2] To see an application of the two systems for the same work, look at the following:

The Ivory Trade: *and the Music of Business at the Van Cliburn International Piano Competition,* by Joseph Horowitz. [This event is held every four years in Ft. Worth, Texas]

LCC class number: ML76.V23

ML	Music Literature
	Special aspects of the subject as a whole
	Prizes, competitions, etc.
76	Individual prizes, competitions, etc., A–Z
.V23	Cutter for Van Cliburn International Piano Competition

DDC class number: 786.2/079/7645315

[Main class]

786	Keyboard, mechanical, electrophonic, percussion instruments
786.2–786.5	Keyboard instruments
786.2–786.4	Keyboard stringed instruments
786.2	Pianos* [*add as instructed under 784–788]

[2nd element]

07	Standard subdivisions (Table 1)
079	Competitions, festivals, awards, financial support
	Add to base number –079 notation 4–9 from Table 2

[3rd element]

	Table 2.Geographic Areas, Periods, Persons
7	North America
76	South central United States Gulf Coast states
764	Texas
764 531	Tarrant County
764 531 5	Fort Worth

This example demonstrates the ability of DDC to represent more facets of a work than the corresponding classification in LCC. We can also observe the way in which the process of notational synthesis is applied. It is interesting how the two systems emphasize different facets of this book. The order of facets in DDC is Piano—Competitions—Geographic location (the second and third elements are derived from two separate tables). LCC brings out two facets only: Competitions—Individual competition (derived by the classifier through instructions in the schedule). There is no facet for piano in this classification number, or for geographic location; on the other hand, DDC provides no direct access for the Van Cliburn competition itself, only indirectly through the geographic facet.

Learning DDC's process of notational synthesis and how to apply it to the classification of music materials is sometimes difficult. It requires a certain level of expertise that can only be gained by careful study of the various volumes of DDC and by working with the system. Because of the enumerative character of LCC, on the other hand, the LC system is relatively easier to master—in many cases, a cataloger only has to consult the schedule itself or the index to find the appropriate class number. But LCC, too, can include a degree of notational synthesis, particularly for certain class numbers in the schedule that require the application of tables.

Another emphasized point is that LCC is really designed for use only in one library. Despite this fact, the Library of Congress's own policies and procedures govern most libraries' technical functions in the U.S. today because of the LC Cataloging Distribution Service and the cooperative activities of LC and national and international organizations, such as the American Library Association. Many of the numbers in the classification schedules for music materials are not applicable for other libraries, especially those with smaller collections or those that are not research-oriented. Most libraries, however, benefit from the availability of LCC, which has remained a flexible and adaptable classification scheme for nearly a century.

The third system, ANSCR, is perhaps the simplest of the three systems. Even though it was designed for only one category of materials, sound recordings, it does have a number of qualities to recommend it over the other two systems for those types of materials and for libraries with relatively small collections. The chief advantage of ANSCR is its "user-friendliness," particularly for browsing. In some ways, it is a very "legalistic" system that requires a certain level of knowledge of the rules for applying the scheme. One of its main drawbacks is the fact that there is no mechanism in place, as with LCC and DDC, for keeping it updated and current. Libraries are pretty well left on their own to adapt ANSCR as their collections grow and change. This is especially important for public libraries, whose collections more frequently reflect changes in popular trends and tastes than those of academic institutions. On the other hand, all libraries, regardless of their focus or type of constituency, routinely make such kinds of adjustments to whatever classification system they adopt. Local practice frequently varies, and despite the type of system that is used, the best libraries are those that respond to their own users' needs without being too strictly bound to existing systems. The common strength of the three systems is that they all share this flexibility and provide a framework for classifying music materials in ways that are logical, intuitive, and adaptable for a wide spectrum of libraries and library users.

NOTES

1. Smiraglia, 91.
2. Libraries are not bound to use the entire number, however, and many institutions have adopted policies that result in simpler numbers for their collections. What is gained in ease of use is lost in lack of specificity.

Class-M Outline

SUBCLASS M, NOTATED MUSIC (PRINTED AND MANUSCRIPT)

SUBCLASS M

1–5000	Music
1.A1–1.A15	Music printed or copies in manuscript in the United States or the colonies before 1860
1.A5–2.3	Collections
2–2.3	Collections of musical sources
3–3.3	Collected works of individual composers
5–1490	Instrumental music
6–175.5	Solo instruments
176	Instrumental music for motion pictures
177–990	Music for two or more solo instruments
180–298.5	Duets
300–386	Trios
400–486	Quartets
500–586	Quintets
600–686	Sextets
700–786	Septets
800–886	Octets
900–986	Nonets and larger combinations of purely instrumental music
990	Chamber music for instruments of the 18th century and earlier
1000–1075	Orchestra
1100–1160	String orchestra
1200–1269	Band
1270	Fife (bugle) and drum music, field music, etc.
1350–1353	Reduced orchestra

1356–1356.2	Dance orchestra and instrumental ensembles
1360	Mandolin and similar orchestras of plucked instruments
1362	Accordion band
1363	Steel band
1365	Minstrel music
1366	Jazz ensembles
1375–1420	Instrumental music for children
1450	Dance music
1470	Chance compositions
1473	Electronic music
1480	Music with color or light apparatus
1490	Music printed before 1700 or copied in manuscript before 1700
1495–5000	Vocal music
1497–1998	Secular vocal music
1500–1527.8	Dramatic music
1528–1529.5	Duets, trios, etc., for solo voices
1530–1546.5	Choruses with orchestra or other ensemble
1547–1600	Choruses, part-songs, etc., with accompaniment of keyboard or other solo instrument, or unaccompanied
1608	Choruses, etc., in tonic sol-fa notation
1609	Unison choruses
1610	Cantatas, choral symphonies, etc., for unaccompanied chorus (secular and sacred) with or without solo voices
1611–1624.8	Songs
1625–1626	Recitations with music
1627–1853	National music
1900–1978	Songs (part and solo) of special character
1985	Musical games
1990–1998	Secular music for children
1999–2199	Sacred vocal music
1999	Collections
2000–2007	Oratorios
2010–2017.6	Services
2018–2019.5	Duets, trios, etc. for solo voices

2020–2036	Choruses, cantatas, etc.
2060–2101.5	Choruses, part-songs, etc., with accompaniment of keyboard or other solo instrument, or unaccompanied
2102–2114.8	Songs
2115–2146	Hymnals. Hymn collections
2147–2188	Liturgy and ritual
2147–2155.6	Roman Catholic Church
2156–2160.87	Orthodox churches
2161–2183	Protestant churches
2184	Other Christian churches
2186–2187	Jewish
2188	Other non-Christian religions
2190–2196	Sacred vocal music for children
2198–2199	Gospel, revival, temperance, etc. songs
5000	Unidentified compositions

SUBCLASS ML, LITERATURE ON MUSIC

1–3930	Literature on music
1–4	Periodicals. Serials
12–21	Directories. Almanacs
25–28	Societies and organizations
32–33	Institutions
35–38	Festivals. Congresses
40–44	Programs
47–54.8	Librettos. Scenarios
62–90	Special aspects
	Including writings on musicians
93–96.5	Manuscripts, autographs
100–109	Dictionaries. Encyclopedias
110–111.5	Music librarianship
112–112.5	Music printing and publishing
112.8–158.8	Bibliography
113–118	International
120	National
132	Graded lists. By medium
135	Manuscripts

136–158	Catalogs. Discography
158.4–158.6	Video recordings
158.8	Computer software
159–3775	History and criticism
162–197	Special periods
162–169	Ancient
169.8–190	Medieval. Renaissance
193–197	1601–
198–360	By region or country
198–239	America
240–325	Europe
330–345	Asia
348	Arab countries
350	Africa
360	Australia, Oceania
385–429	Biography
430–455	Composition
459–1380	Instruments and instrumental music
465–471	By period
475–547	By region or country
475–486	America
489–522	Europe
525–541	Asia
544	Africa
547	Australia, Oceania
548	Jews
549–1093	Instruments
549.8–649	Organ
649.8–747	Piano, clavichord, harpsichord, etc.
749.5–927	Bowed string instruments
929–990	Wind instruments
999–1015	Plucked instruments
1030–1049	Percussion instruments
1049.8–1091	Mechanical and other instruments
1091.8–1093	Electronic instruments
1100–1165	Chamber music
1200–1270	Orchestra
1299–1354	Band

SUBCLASS MT, MUSICAL INSTRUCTION AND STUDY

280–298	Viola
300–318	Violoncello
320–334	Double bass
339–533	Wind instruments
340–359	Flute
360–379	Oboe
380–392	Clarinet (A, B-flat, C, E-flat, etc.)
400–415	Bassoon
418	Brass instruments
420–432	Horn
440–456	Trumpet
460–472	Trombone
480–488	Tuba
500–510	Saxophone
539–654	Plucked instruments
540–557	Harp
560–570	Banjo
580–599	Guitar
600–612	Mandolin
620–634	Zither
640–654	Lute, balalaika, etc.
655–725	Percussion and other instruments
728–728.3	Chamber music
730	Orchestra
733–733.6	Band
740–810	Instrumental techniques for children
820–915	Singing and vocal technique
825–850	Systems and methods
855–883	Special techniques
898–915	Techniques for children
918–948	School music
955–956	Musical theater

Selected Bibliography

Ayer, Clarence W. "Shelf Classification of Music." *Library Journal* 27 (1902): 5-11.

Bardwell, W. A. "A Library of Music." *Library Journal* 12 (1887): 159.

Barkey, Patrick T. "Phono-record Filing System." *Library Journal* 82 (1957): 2514.

Benton, Rita. "The Nature of Music and Some Implications for the University Music Library." *Fontes Artis Musicae* 23 (1976): 53-60.

Bradley, Carol June. *The Dickinson Classification: A Cataloging & Classification Manual for Music: Including a Reprint of the George Sherman Dickinson Classification of Musical Compositions.* Carlisle, Pa.: Carlisle Books, 1968.

———. "The Dickinson Classification for Music: An Introduction." *Fontes Artis Musicae* (1972): 13-22.

———. *Manual of Music Librarianship.* Ann Arbor, Mich.: Music Library Association, 1966.

———. *Reader in Music Librarianship.* Washington, D.C.: Microcard Edition Books, 1973.

Brown, James Duff. "Cataloguing of Music." *The Library*, series I (1897): 82-84.

Buth, Olga. "Scores and Recordings." *Library Trends* 23 (1975): 427-50.

Cataloger's Desktop. Issue 2. Washington, D.C.: Library of Congress, Cataloging Distribution Service, 2001.

Chan, Lois Mai. *Cataloging and Classification: An Introduction.* New York: McGraw-Hill, 1981.

———. *A Guide to the Library of Congress Classification.* 5th ed. Englewood, Colo.: Libraries Unlimited, 1999.

Chan, Lois Mai, John P. Comaromi, Joan S. Mitchell, and Mohinder P. Satija. *Dewey Decimal Classification: A Practical Guide.* 2d ed, rev. for DDC 21. Albany, N.Y.: Forest Press, 1996.

Classification Plus. Issue 2. Washington, D.C.: Library of Congress, Cataloging Distribution Service, 2001.

Cutter, Charles Ammi. "Shelf Classification of Music." *Library Journal* 27 (1902): 68-72.

Dewey, Melvil. *A Classification and Subject Index for Cataloging and Arranging the Books and Pamphlets of a Library.* Amherst, Mass.: 1876. Reprint, *Dewey Decimal Classification Centennial 1876-1976.* N.p.: Forest Press Division, Lake Placid Education Foundation, 1976.

———. "Decimal Classification Beginnings." *Library Journal* 45 (1920): 151-54.

———. *Dewey Decimal Classification and Relative Index.* 19th ed., edited under the direction of Benjamin A. Custer. Albany, N.Y.: Forest Press, 1979.

———. *Dewey Decimal Classification and Relative Index.* 20th ed. Edited by John P. Comaromi. Albany, N.Y.: Forest Press, 1989.

———. *Dewey Decimal Classification and Relative Index.* 21st ed. Edited by Joan S. Mitchell. Albany, N.Y.: Forest Press, 1996.

Dickinson, George Sherman. *Classification of Musical Compositions: A Decimal-Symbol System.* Poughkeepsie, N.Y.: Vassar College, 1938.

Foley, Edward, ed. *Worship Music: A Concise Dictionary.* Collegeville, Minn.: The Liturgical Press, 2000.

Gaeddert, Barbara. *The Classification and Cataloging of Sound Recordings: 1933-1980: An Annotated Bibliography.* 2d ed. Philadelphia: Music Library Association, 1981.

Gorman, Michael, and Paul W. Winkler, ed. *Anglo-American Cataloguing Rules.* 2d ed., 1988 revision. Chicago: American Library Association, 1988.

Hamm, Charles. *Yesterdays: Popular Song in America.* New York: W.W. Norton, 1979.

Hansen, Linda L. *ANSCR Supplement 1988.* Gardena, Calif.: Professional Media Service Corp., 1988.

Holoman, D. Kern. *Catalogue of the Works of Hector Berlioz.* New York: Bärenreiter, 1987.

Hornbostel, Erich M. von, and Curt Sachs. "Classification of Musical Instruments." Translated from the original German by Anthony Baines and Klaus P. Wachsmann. *Galpin Society Journal* 14 (1961): 3-29.

LaMontagne, Leo E. *American Library Classification: With Special Reference to the Library of Congress.* Hamden, Conn.: Shoe String Press, 1961.

Library of Congress. *Subject Cataloging Manual: Shelflisting.* 2nd ed. Washington, D.C.: Library of Congress Cataloging Policy and Support Office, 1995.

———. *Subject Cataloging Manual: Classification.* Washington, D.C.: Library of Congress Cataloging Distribution Service, 1992.

———. *Library of Congress Classification: M: Music and Books on Music.* 3d ed. Washington, D.C.: Library of Congress. Subject Cataloging Division, 1978.

——. *Library of Congress Classification. M, Music and Books on Music.* 1998 ed. Washington, D.C.: Library of Congress Cataloging Distribution Service, 1999.

McColvin, Lionel Roy, and Harold Reeves. *Music Libraries.* London: Grafton, 1937.

Music Library Association. Cataloging and Classification Committee. *SLACC: The Partial Use of the Shelf List as a Classed Catalog.* Don Seibert, Chairman. MLA Technical Reports, no. 1. Ann Arbor, Mich.: Music Library Association, 1973.

Osborn, Jeanne. *Dewey Decimal Classification, 20th Edition: A Study Manual.* Revised and edited by John P. Comaromi. Englewood, Colo.: Libraries Unlimited, 1991.

Poultney, David. *Dictionary of Western Church Music.* Chicago: American Library Association, 1991.

Redfern, Brian. *Organising Music in Libraries.* London: Bingley, 1966.

Saheb-Ettaba, Caroline, and Roger B. McFarland. *ANSCR: The Alpha-Numeric System for Classification of Sound Recordings.* Williamsport, Pa.: Bro-Dart Publishing Co., 1969.

Smiraglia, Richard. *Music Cataloging: The Bibliographic Control of Printed and Recorded Music in Libraries.* Englewood, Colo.: Libraries Unlimited, 1989.

——. *Shelflisting Music: Guidelines for Use with the Library of Congress Classification: M.* MLA Technical Reports, no. 9. Philadelphia: Music Library Association, 1981.

Stevenson, Gordon. "Classification Chaos." *Library Journal,* October 15, 1963. Reprinted in *Reader in Music Librarianship,* ed. Carol June Bradley, 274-78. Washington, D.C.: Microcard Editions Books, 1973.

Wursten, Richard, comp. *In Celebration of Revised 780: Music in the Dewey Decimal Classification, Edition 20.* MLA Technical Reports, no. 19. Canton, Mass.: Music Library Association, 1990.

Wynar, Bohdan S. *Introduction to Cataloging and Classification,* 7th ed. by Arlene G. Taylor. Littleton, Colo.: Libraries Unlimited, 1985.

Index

Page numbers in italics indicate figures.

About tl

Mark McKnight is associate head of the music library at
of North Texas (UNT), where he coordinates music cat
ties. He also teaches courses in the UNT College of Mus
Theory, History, and Ethnomusicology, as well as in the
brary and Information Science. Prior to his appointment a
music and audiovisual catalog librarian at Loyola Univ
Orleans. He holds a Ph.D. in music history from Louisi;
versity and an M.S. in library and information science fro
sity of Illinois, Urbana-Champaign. McKnight is active in
brary Association, where he has held a number of c
involved with the Music Thesaurus Project. He has writte
extensively in his areas of scholarly interest and research,
nineteenth-century American music criticism, early Ameri
sic, and the music of Louisiana and New Orleans.

About the Author

Mark McKnight is associate head of the music library at the University of North Texas (UNT), where he coordinates music cataloging activities. He also teaches courses in the UNT College of Music Division of Theory, History, and Ethnomusicology, as well as in the School of Library and Information Science. Prior to his appointment at UNT, he was music and audiovisual catalog librarian at Loyola University in New Orleans. He holds a Ph.D. in music history from Louisiana State University and an M.S. in library and information science from the University of Illinois, Urbana-Champaign. McKnight is active in the Music Library Association, where he has held a number of offices and is involved with the Music Thesaurus Project. He has written and lectured extensively in his areas of scholarly interest and research, which include nineteenth-century American music criticism, early American sheet music, and the music of Louisiana and New Orleans.